After Auschwitz

Responses to the Holocaust in Contemporary Art

DEDICATION

This book and this exhibition are lovingly dedicated to the memory of my father Louis Bohm, in the knowledge that he understood my wish to pay tribute to the family in Poland I never knew.

Monica Bohm-Duchen

Responses to the Holocaust in Contemporary Art

After Auschwitz

Edited by Monica Bohm-Duchen

Northern Centre for Contemporary Art, Sunderland
in association with Lund Humphries, London

farca

First published in Great Britain in 1995 by
Northern Centre for Contemporary Art, Sunderland
in association with
Lund Humphries Publishers Limited
Park House
1 Russell Gardens
London NW11 9NN

on the occasion of the exhibition
After Auschwitz: Responses to the Holocaust in Contemporary Art
Royal Festival Hall, London   26 February – 17 April 1995
Manchester City Art Gallery   13 May – 2 July 1995
Angel Row Gallery, Nottingham   July – August 1995
Northern Centre for Contemporary Art, Sunderland   Autumn 1995
Edinburgh City Art Centre   Winter 1995

and *After Auschwitz: Installations*
Imperial War Museum, London   23 February – 29 May 1995

British Library Cataloguing in Publication Data
A catalogue record of this book is available from
the British Library

ISBN 0 85331 666 X

Designed by Alan Bartram
Made and printed in Great Britain
by BAS Printers Limited
Over Wallop, Hampshire

FRONTISPIECE
Henning Langenheim, *Buchenwald 1991: Panorama* (Cat.37)

Contents

Acknowledgements

A project such as this one has been a challenge on many levels – and had it not been for the help and support of a few individuals, it would have seemed at times a lonely task. To those few – Glenn Sujo, Lily R. Markiewicz, my parents Dorothy and Louis Bohm and my husband Michael Duchen – I extend my heartfelt thanks.

I should also like to thank the following people for their willingness to share their knowledge with me: in Israel, Professor Ziva Amishai-Maisels, Avi Hurwitz and Irit Salmon-Livne; in North America, Dr Stephen Feinstein; and in Germany, Professor Detlef Hoffmann and Dr Jochen Spielmann. Other people – notably, Janus Avivson, Benedict Brogan, Roman Halter, Ben Helfgott, Ruth Kohn-Corman, Anthony Newton, Phyllis Rapp and Liesel Schwab – have helped in more practical ways, and I am grateful to them too.

Financial support has been received from a number of sources, to whom the project is deeply indebted. As well as those benefactors who have preferred to remain anonymous, I should like to thank the following individuals: Sidney and Elizabeth Corob, Jack Goldhill, Arnold Horwell, Robert Lewin, M. J. Margulies, Cyril Stein and Fred S. Worms; also, the Embassy of the Federal Republic of Germany, the Rayne Foundation and the Leopold Muller Estate (and E. Michael Garston in particular). In addition, the practical assistance of GSI Cargo Systems Ltd has been invaluable.

One of the rewards of working on this exhibition has been the opportunity to meet with so many artists of integrity. It hardly needs saying that selecting the artists for inclusion was a difficult and delicate task. Lily Markiewicz and Mike Hill were both closely involved in this process; yet the choice was ultimately a personal one, for which I must take full responsibility. Fortunately, I have been able, in my essay in the present volume, to refer to many more artists than I was able to include in the exhibition. In any event, I am grateful to all the artists who gave me their time, as well as those I never met, but who were kind enough to send me information about their work.

Lastly, I should like to thank Mike Hill, Director of the Northern Centre for Contemporary Art in Sunderland, who invited me to curate the exhibition approximately four years ago, for having the vision and the courage to commission such a project in the first place.

MONICA BOHM-DUCHEN

Photographic Credits

The authors and the publishers thank the following for permission to reproduce works, or for providing photographs:
AP/World Wide Photos Fig.50
Avigdor Arikha, Paris Fig.10
The Art Institute of Chicago Col.Fig.27
Collection, The Museum of Modern Art, New York Fig.22
DACS, London Figs 21, 22, 24, 25; Col.Figs 27, 29, 33
Estate of Nathan Rapoport Fig.47
Esther Gerz Fig.36
Jochen Gerz Col.Fig.52
Hans Haacke Fig.39
Joram Harel, Vienna Col.Fig.31

Horst Hoheisel Figs 43, 44
Israel Museum, Jerusalem Fig.78; Col.Fig.34
Jason & Rhodes Gallery, London Col.Fig.65
Jewish Historical Institute, Warsaw Fig.7
Kulturbehörde, Hamburg Fig.41
Leo Castelli Gallery, New York Col.Fig.28
J. Mostowik Fig.45
Eigil Nansen, Oslo Fig.5
National Gallery of Canada, Ottawa Col.Fig.72
Philadelphia Museum of Art Fig.35 (Given by R. Sturgis and Marion B. F. Ingersoll)
PHOTO R.M.N., Paris Col.Fig.33
Dean Powell Col.Figs 60, 61

David Reynolds Col.Fig.68
Sachsenhausen Museum Fig.5
Artur Starewicz, Warsaw Fig.57
Boris Taslitzky, Paris Figs 1, 2, 12, 14
Tate Gallery, London Col.Fig.32
Time Life Magazine Fig.4
James E. Young Figs 37, 38, 40, 42, 46, 48, 49; Col.Figs 51, 53

The authors and publishers have made every effort to trace the copyright holders or owners of works and photographs. If any institutions or individuals have been incorrectly credited, or if there are any omissions, we would be glad to be notified so that the necessary corrections can be made in any reprint.

George Steiner   *For Elie Wiesel*

A Kind of Survivor

Not literally. Due to my father's foresight (he had shown it when leaving Vienna in 1924), I came to America in January 1940, during the phoney war. We left France, where I was born and brought up, in safety. So I happened not to be there when the names were called out. I did not stand in the public square with the other children, those I had grown up with. Or see my father and mother disappear when the train doors were torn open. But in another sense I am a survivor, and not intact. If I am often out of touch with my own generation, if that which haunts me and controls my habits of feeling strikes many of those I should be intimate and working with in my present world as remotely sinister and artificial, it is because the black mystery of what happened in Europe is to me indivisible from my own identity. Precisely because I was not there, because an accident of good fortune struck my name from the roll.

Often the children went alone, or held the hands of strangers. Sometimes parents saw them pass and did not dare call out their names. And they went, of course, not for anything they had done or said. But because their parents existed before them. The crime of being one's children. During the Nazi period it knew no absolution, no end. Does it now? Somewhere the determination to kill Jews, to harass them from the earth simply because they *are*, is always alive. Ordinarily, the purpose is muted, or appears in trivial spurts – the obscenity daubed on the front door, the brick through the shop window. But there are, even now, places where the murderous intent might grow heavy: in Russia, in parts of North Africa, in certain countries of Latin America. Where tomorrow? So, at moments, when I see my children in the room, or imagine that I hear them breathing in the still of the house, I grow afraid. Because I have put on their backs a burden of ancient loathing and set savagery at their heels. Because it may be that I will be able to do no more than the parents of the dead children to guard them.

That fear lies near the heart of the way in which I think of myself as a Jew. To have been a European Jew in the first half of the twentieth century was to pass sentence on one's own children, to force upon them a condition almost beyond rational understanding. And which may recur. I have to think that – it is the vital clause – so long as remembrance is real. Perhaps we Jews walk closer to our children than other men; try as they may, they cannot leap out of our shadow.

This is my self-definition. Mine, because I cannot speak for any other Jew. All of us obviously have something in common. We do tend to recognise one another wherever we meet, nearly at a glance, by some common trick of feeling, by the darkness we carry. But each of us must hammer it out for himself. That is the real meaning of the Diaspora, of the wide scattering and thinning of belief.

To the Orthodox my definition must seem desperate and shallow. Entire communities stayed close-knit to the end. There were children who did not cry out but said *Shema Yisroel* and kept their eyes wide open because His kingdom lay just a step over the charnel pit (not as many as is sometimes said, but there *were*). To the strong believer the torture and massacre of six million is one chapter – one only – in the millennial dialogue between God and the people He has so terribly chosen. Though Judaism lacks a dogmatic eschatology (it leaves to the individual the imagining of transcendence), the Orthodox can meditate on the camps as a forecourt of God's house, as an almost intolerable but manifest mystery of His will. When he teaches his children the prayers and rites (my own access to these was that of history, not of present faith), when they sing at his side at the high holidays, the pious Jew looks on them not with fear, not as hostages that bear the doom of his love, but in pride and rejoicing. Through them the bread shall remain blessed and the wine sanctified. They are alive not because of a clerical oversight in a Gestapo office, but because they no less than the dead are part of God's truth. Without them history would stand empty. The

Reproduced from George Steiner, Language and Silence, *Faber & Faber, 1979. This essay was written in 1965, and should be read in the context of the time.*

Orthodox Jew defines himself (as I cannot) in the rich life of his prayer, of an inheritance both tragic and resplendent. He harvests the living echo of his own being from the voices of his community and the holiness of the word. His children are like the night turned to song.

The Orthodox Jew would not only deny me the right to speak for him, pointing to my lack of knowledge and communion; he would say, 'You are not like us, you are a Jew outwardly, in name only'. Exactly. But the Nazis made of the mere name necessary and sufficient cause. They did not ask whether one had ever been to synagogue, whether one's children knew any Hebrew. The anti-Semite is no theologian; but his definition is inclusive. So we would all have gone together, the Orthodox and I. And the gold teeth would have come out of our dead mouths, song or no song.

Two passages from Exodus help the mind grasp enormity. Perhaps they are mistranslations or archaic shards interpolated in the canonic text. But they help me as do poetry and metaphor, by giving imaginative logic to grim possibility. Exodus IV, 24 tells how God sought to kill Moses: 'And it came to pass by the way in the inn, that the Lord met him and sought to kill him.' I gloss this to mean that God suffers gusts of murderous exasperation at the Jews, towards a people who have made Him a responsible party to history and to the grit of man's condition. He may not have wished to be involved; the people may have chosen Him, in the oasis at Kadesh, and thrust upon Him the labours of justice and right anger. It may have been the Jew who caught Him by the skirt, insisting on contact and dialogue. Perhaps before either God or living man was ready for proximity. So as in marriage, or the bond between father and child, there are moments when love is changed to something very much like itself, pure hatred.

The second text is Exodus XXXIII, 22-3. Moses is once more on Sinai, asking for a new set of tablets (we have always been nagging Him, demanding justice and reason twice over). There follows a strange ceremony of recognition: 'And it shall come to pass, while my glory passeth by, that I will put thee in a cleft of the rock, and will cover thee with my hand while I pass by: And I will take away mine hand, and thou shalt see my back parts: but my face shall not be seen.' This may be the decisive clue: God can turn His back. There may be minutes or millennia – is our time His? – in which He does not see man, in which He is looking the *other way*. Why? Perhaps because through some minute, hideous error of design the universe is too large for His surveillance, because somewhere there is a millionth of an inch, it need be no more, out of His line of sight. So He must turn to look there also. When God's back parts are towards man, history is Belsen.

If the Orthodox Jew cannot allow my definition, or this use of the holy word as metaphor and paradox, neither can the Zionist and the Israeli. They do not deny the catastrophe, but they know that it bore splendid fruit. Out of the horror came the new chance. The State of Israel is undeniably a part of the legacy of German mass murder. Hope and the will to action spring from the capacity of the human mind to forget, from the instinct for necessary oblivion. The Israeli Jew cannot look back too often; his must be the dreams not of night but of day, the forward dreams. Let the dead bury the mounds of the dead. His history is not theirs; it has just begun. To someone like myself, the Israeli Jew might say: 'Why aren't you here? If you fear for the lives of your children, why not send them here and let them grow up amid their own kind? Why burden them with your own perhaps literary, perhaps masochistic, remembrance of disaster? This is their future. They have a right to it. We need all the brains and sinews we can get. We're not working for ourselves alone. There isn't a Jew in the world who doesn't hold his head higher because of what we've done here, because Israel exists.'

Which is obviously true. The status of the Jew everywhere has altered a little, the image he carries of himself has a new straightness of back, because Israel has shown that Jews can handle modern weapons, that they can fly jets, and turn desert into orchard. When he is pelted in Argentina or mocked in Kiev, the Jewish child knows that there is a corner of the earth where he is master, where the gun is his. If Israel were to be destroyed, no Jew would escape unscathed. The shock of failure, the need and harrying of those seeking refuge, would reach out to implicate even the most indifferent, the most anti-Zionist.

So why not go? Why not leave the various lands in which we still live, it seems to me, as more or less accepted guests? Many Russian Jews might go if they could. North African Jews are doing so even at the price of destitution. The Jews of South Africa may before too long be forced to the same resolve. So why don't I go, who am at liberty, whose children could grow up far from the spoor of the inhuman past? I don't know if there is a good answer. But there is a reason.

If the way I think of my Jewishness will appear unacceptable or self-defeating to the Orthodox and the Israeli, it will also seem remote and over-dramatised to most American Jews. The idea that Jews everywhere have been maimed by the European catastrophe, that the massacre has left all who survived (even if they were nowhere near the actual scene) off balance, as does the tearing of a limb, is one which American Jews can understand in an intellectual sense. But I don't find that it has immediate personal relevance. The relationship of the American Jew to recent history is subtly and radically different from that of the European. By its very finality, the Holocaust justified every previous impulse of immigration. All who had left Europe to establish the new Jewish communities in America were proved terribly right. The Jewish soldier who went to the Europe of his fathers came better armed, technologically more efficient than his murderous enemy. The few Jews he found alive were out of a hideous but spectral world, like a nightmare in a foreign tongue. In America,

Jewish parents listen at night for their children; but it is to make sure that the car is back in the garage, not because there is a mob out. It cannot happen in Scarsdale.

I am not sure, not completely (this is precisely where I am an outsider). Most American Jews are aware of anti-Semitism in specialised areas of life – the club, the holiday resort, the residential district, the professional guild. But in comparative terms, it tends to be mild, perhaps because America, unlike Europe or Russia, has no history of guilt towards the Jew. The size and human wealth of the American Jewish community are such, moreover, that a Jew need hardly go outside his own sphere to enjoy American life at its best and freest. The principal dynamism of American life, however, is a middle- and lower-middle-class conformity, an enforcing consensus of taste and ideal. Nearly by definition, the Jew stands in the way of uniform coherence. Economic, social or political stress tend to make this latent disparity – the hostile recognition and reciprocal self-awareness of 'difference' – more acute. Depression or a drastic increase in unemployment would isolate the status of the Jew, focusing resentment on his prosperity and on the ostentatious forms that prosperity has taken in certain aspects of Jewish life. The struggle over Negro rights, which is coming to overshadow so much of American life, has obvious bearing. Among urban Negroes anti-Semitism is often open and raw. It can be used by the Negro as a basis of temporary alliance with other underprivileged or resentful elements in the white community. Beyond these possibilities lies the larger pattern: the stiffening of consensus, the increasing concentration of American values in a standardised moralistic nationalism.

I agree that American anti-Semitism will stay mild and covert. So long as the economy expands and the racial conflict can be kept in tolerable bounds. So long as Israel is viable and can offer refuge. This is probably the root condition. The support given to Israel by the American Jewish community is both thoroughly generous and thoroughly self-interested. If a new wave of immigration occurred, if the Russian or Tunisian Jew came knocking at America's door, the status of American Jewry would be immediately affected.

These complex safeguards and conditions of acceptance can break down. America is no more immune than any other nationalistic, professedly Christian society from the contagion of anti-Semitism. In a crisis of resentment or exclusion, even the more assimilated would be driven back to our ancient legacy of fear. Though he might have forgotten it and turned Unitarian (a characteristic half-way house), Mr Harrison's neighbours would remind him that his father was called Horowitz. To deny this is to assert that in America human character and historical forces have undergone some miraculous change – a utopian claim which the actual development of American life in the twentieth century has more than once rebuked.

Nevertheless, the sense I have of the Jew as a man who looks on his children with a dread remembrance of helplessness and an intimation of future, murderous possibility, is a very personal, isolated one. It does not relate to much that is now alive and hopeful. But it is not wholly negative either. I mean to include in it far more than the naked precedent of ruin. That which has been destroyed – the large mass of life so mocked, so hounded to oblivion that even the names are gone and the prayer for the dead can have no exact foothold – embodied a particular genius, a quality of intelligence and feeling which none of the major Jewish communities now surviving has preserved or recaptured. Because I feel that specific inheritance urgent in my own reflexes, in the work I try to do, I am a kind of survivor.

In respect of *secular* thought and achievement, the period of Jewish history which ended at Auschwitz surpassed even the brilliant age of co-existence in Islamic Spain. During roughly a century, from the emancipation of the ghettos by the French Revolution and Napoleon to the time of Hitler, the Jew took part in the moral, intellectual and artistic noon of bour-geois Europe. The long confinement of the ghetto, the sharpening of wit and nervous insight against the whetstone of persecution, had accumulated large reserves of consciousness. Released into the light, a certain Jewish élite, and the wider middle-class circle which took pride and interest in its accomplishments, quickened and complicated the entire contour of Western thought. To every domain they brought radical imaginings; more specifically, the more gifted Jews repossessed certain crucial elements of classic European civilisation in order to make them new and problematic. All this is commonplace; as is the inevitable observation that the tenor of modernity, the shapes of awareness and query by which we order our lives are, in substantial measure, the work of Marx, Freud and Einstein.

What is far more difficult to show, though it seems to me undeniable, is the extent to which a common heritage of fairly recent emancipation, a particular bias of rational feeling – specialised in origin but broadening out to become the characteristic modern note – informs their distinct, individual genius. In all three, we discern a mastering impulse to visionary logic, to imagination in the abstract, as if the long banishment of the Eastern and European Jew from material action had given to thought a dramatic autonomy. The intimation of an energy of imagination at once sensuous and abstract, the release of the Jewish sensibility into a world dangerously new, unencumbered by reverence, is similarly at work in the subversions of Schoenberg and Kafka, and in the mathematics of Cantor. It relates Wittgenstein's *Tractatus* to that of Spinoza.

Without the contribution made by the Jews between 1830 and 1930, Western culture would be obviously different and diminished. At the same time, of course, it was his collision with established European values, with classic modes of art and argument, which compelled the emancipated Jew to define his range and identity. In this collision, in the attempt to achieve poise in an essentially borrowed milieu, the converted Jew or half-Jew, the Jew whose relation to his own past grew covert or antagonistic – Heine, Bergson, Hofmannsthal, Proust – played a particularly subtle and creative role.

Those who helped define and shared in this *Central European Humanism* (each of the three terms carrying its full charge of implication and meaning) showed characteristic traits, characteristic habits of taste and recognition. They had a quick way with languages. Heine is the first, perhaps the only great poet whom it is difficult to locate in any single linguistic sensibility. The habits of reference of this European Jewish generation often point to the Greek and Latin classics; but these were seen through the special focus of Winckelmann, Lessing and Goethe. An almost axiomatic sense of Goethe's transcendent stature, of the incredible ripeness and humanity of his art, colours the entire European-Jewish enlightenment, and continues to mark its few survivors (Goethe's fragment *On Nature* converted Freud from an early interest in law to the study of the biological sciences). The Central European Jewish bourgeoisie was frequently intimate with the plays of Shakespeare and assumed, rightly, that the performance of Shakespearean drama in Vienna, Munich or Berlin (often acted and staged by Jews) more than matched what could be found in England. It read Balzac and Stendhal (one recalls Léon Blum's pioneer study of Beyle), Tolstoy, Ibsen and Zola. But it often read them in a special, almost heightened context. The Jews who welcomed Scandinavian drama and the Russian novel tended to see in the new realism and iconoclasm of literature a part of the general liberation of spirit. Zola was not only the explorer of erotic and economic realities, as were Freud, Weininger or Marx: he was the champion of Dreyfus.

The relationship of Jewish consciousness to Wagner was passionate, though uneasy. We see late instances of this duality in the musicology of Adorno and the fiction of Werfel. It recognised in Wagner the radicalism and histrionic tactics of a great outsider. It caught in Wagner's anti-Semitism a queer, intimate note, and gave occasional heed to the stubborn myth that Wagner was himself of Jewish descent. Being new to the plastic arts, hence beautifully free and empiric in its responses, Jewish taste, in the guise of dealer, patron and critic, backed Impressionism and the blaze of the modern. Through Reinhardt and Piscator it renovated the theatre; through Gustav Mahler the relations between serious music and society. In its golden period, from 1870 to 1914, then again in the 1920s, the Jewish leaven gave to Prague and Berlin, to Vienna and Paris a specific vitality of feeling and expression, an atmosphere both quintessentially European and 'off-centre'. The nuance of spirit is delicately mocked and made memorable in the unquiet hedonism, in the erudite urbanity of Proust's Swann.

Almost nothing of it survives. This is what makes my own, almost involuntary, identification with it so shadowy a condition. European Jewry and its intelligentsia were caught between two waves of murder, Nazism and Stalinism. The implication of the European and Russian Jew in Marxism had natural causes. As has often been said, the dream of a secular millennium – which is still alive in Georg Lukács and the master historian of hope, Ernst Bloch – relates the social utopia of communism to the messianic tradition. For both Jew and communist, history is a scenario of gradual humanisation, an immensely difficult attempt by man to become man. In both modes of feeling there is an obsession with the prophetic authority of moral or historical law, with the right reading of canonic revelations. But from Eduard Bernstein to Trotsky, from Isaac Babel to Pasternak, the involvement of the Jewish personality in communism and the Russian revolution follows an ironic pattern. Nearly invariably it ends in dissent or heresy – in that heresy which claims to be orthodox because it is seeking to restore the betrayed meaning of Marx (the Polish Marxist Adam Schaff would be a contemporary instance of this 'Talmudic revisionism'). As Stalinism turned to nationalism and technocracy – the new

Russia of the managerial middle class has its precise origins in the Stalinist period – the revolutionary intelligentsia went to the wall. The Jewish Marxist, the Trotskyite, the socialist fellow-traveller were trapped in the ruins of utopia. The Jew who had joined communism in order to fight the Nazis, the Jewish communist who had broken with the party after the purge trials, fell into the net of the Hitler–Stalin pact.

In one of the vilest episodes in modern history, the militia and police of European appeasement and European totalitarianism collaborated in handing over Jews. The French delivered to the Gestapo those who had fled from Spain and Germany. Himmler and the GPU exchanged anti-Stalinist and anti-Nazi Jews for further torture and elimination. One thinks of Walter Benjamin – one of the most brilliant representatives of radical humanism – committing suicide lest the French or Spanish border-guards hand him over to the invading SS; of Buber-Neumann whose widow was nearly hounded to death by Stalinist cadres *inside* a Nazi concentration camp; of a score of others trapped between the Nazi and the Stalinist hunter (the memoirs of Victor Serge close with the roll of their several and hideous deaths). Which bestial bargain and exchange at the frontier made eloquent the decision to hound the Jew out of European history. But also the peculiar dignity of his torment. Perhaps we can define ourselves thus: *The Jews are a people whom totalitarian barbarism must choose for its hatred.*

A certain number escaped. It is easily demonstrable that much important work in American scholarship in the period from 1934 to *c.*1955, in the arts, in the exact and social sciences, is the afterlife of the Central European renaissance and embodied the talent of the refugee. But the particular cast of the American Jewish intelligence on native ground, which I first met at the University of Chicago in the late 1940s, and which now plays so obviously powerful a role in American intellectual and artistic life, is something very different. There is little of Karl Kraus's notion of style and humane literacy in, say, *Partisan Review.* Kraus is very nearly a touchstone. Ask a man if he has heard of him or read his *Literature and Lies.* If so, he is probably one of the survivors.

In Kraus, as in Kafka and Hermann Broch, there is a mortal premonition and finality. Broch, who seems to me the major European novelist after Joyce and Mann, is a defining figure. His *The Death of Virgil*, his philosophic essays, are an epilogue to humanism. They focus on the deed which should dominate our rational lives so far as we still conduct them, which should persistently bewilder our sense of self – the turn of civilisation to mass murder. Like certain parables of Kafka and the epistemology of the early Wittgenstein, the art of Broch goes near the edge of necessary silence. It asks whether speech, whether the shapes of moral judgement and imagination which the Judaic-Hellenic tradition founds on the authority of the word, are viable in the face of the inhuman. Is the poet's verse not an insult to the naked cry? Broch died in America in a strange, vital solitude, giving voice to a civilisation, to an inheritance of humane striving, already done to death.

The humanism of the European Jew lies in literal ash. In the accent of survivors – Hannah Arendt, Ernst Bloch, T. W. Adorno, Erich Kahler, Lévi-Strauss – whose interests and commitments are, of course, diverse, you will hear a common note as of desolation. Yet it is these voices which seem to me contemporary, whose work and context of reference are indispensable to an understanding of the philosophic, political, aesthetic roots of the inhuman; of the paradox that modern barbarism sprang in some intimate, perhaps necessary way, from the very core and locale of humanistic civilisation. If this is so, why do we try to teach, to write, to contend for literacy? Which question, and I know of none more urgent, or the idiom in which it is put, probably puts the asker thirty years out of date – on either side of the present.

As do certain other questions, increasingly muted and out of focus. Yet which cannot go unasked if we are to argue the values and possibilities of our culture. I mean the general complicity in the massacre. There were superb exceptions (in Denmark, Norway, Bulgaria), but the tale is sordid and much of it remains an ugly riddle. At a time when 9000 Jews were being exterminated *each day*, neither the RAF nor the US Air Force bombed the ovens or sought to blow open the camps (as Mosquitoes, flying low, had broken wide a prison in France to liberate agents of the Maquis). Though the Jewish and Polish underground made desperate pleas, though the German bureaucracy made little secret of the fact that the 'final solution' depended on rail transport, the lines to Belsen and Auschwitz were not bombed. Why? The question has been asked of Churchill and Harris. Has there been an adequate answer? When the *Wehrmacht* and *Waffen-SS* poured into Russia, Soviet intelligence quickly noted the mass killing of the Jews. Stalin forbade any public announcement of the fact. Here again, the reasons are obscure. He may not have wanted a rekindling of separate Jewish consciousness; he may have feared implicit reference to his own anti-Semitic policies. Whatever the cause, many Jews who could have fled eastward stayed behind unknowing. Later on, in the Ukraine, local gangs helped the Germans round up those who cowered in cellars and woods.

I wonder what would have happened if Hitler had played the game after Munich, if he had simply said, 'I will make no move outside the Reich so long as I am allowed a free hand inside my borders'. Dachau, Buchenwald and Theresienstadt would have operated in the middle of twentieth-century European civilisation until the last Jew in reach had been made soap. There would have been brave words on Trafalgar Square and in Carnegie Hall, to audiences diminishing and bored. Society might, on occasion, have boycotted German wines. But no foreign power would have taken action. Tourists would have crowded the *Autobahn* and spas of the Reich, passing near but not too near the death-camps as we now pass Portuguese jails or Greek prison-islands. There would have been numerous pundits and journalists to assure us that rumours were exaggerated, that Dachau had pleasant walks. And the Red Cross would have sent Christmas parcels.

Below his breath, the Jew asks of his gentile neighbour: 'If you had known, would you have cried in the face of God and man that this hideousness must stop? Would you have made some attempt to get my children out? Or planned a ski-ing party to Garmisch?' The Jew is a living reproach.

Men are accomplices to that which leaves them indifferent. It is this fact which must, I think, make the Jew wary inside Western culture, which must lead him to re-examine ideals and historical traditions that, certainly in Europe, had enlisted the best of his hopes and genius. The house of civilisation proved no shelter.

But then, I have never been sure about houses. Perforce, the Jew has often been wanderer and guest. He can buy an old manse and plant a garden. An anxious pastoralism is a distinctive part of the attempt of many American middle-class and intellectual Jews to assimilate to the Anglo-Saxon background. But I wonder whether it's quite the same. The dolls in the attic were not ours; the ghosts have a rented air. Characteristically, Marx, Freud, Einstein end their lives far from their native ground, in exile or refuge. The Jew has his anchorage not in place but in time, in his highly developed sense of history as personal context. Six thousand years of self-awareness are a homeland.

I find that the edge of strangeness and temporary habitation carries over into language, though here again my experience is obviously different from that of the native-born American Jew. European Jews learned languages quickly; often they had to as they wandered. But a final 'at homeness' may elude us, that unconscious, immemorial intimacy which a man has with his native idiom as he does with the rock, earth and ash of his acre. Hence the particular strategies of the two greatest European Jewish writers.

Heine's German, as Adorno has pointed out, is a brilliantly personal, European idiom on which his fluent knowledge of French exercised a constant pressure. Kafka wrote German as if it were all bone, as if none of the enveloping texture of colloquialism, of historical and regional overtone, had been allowed him. He used each word as if he had borrowed it at high interest. Many great actors are or have been Jews. Language passes *through* them, and they shape it almost too well, like a treasure acquired, not inalienable. This may be pertinent also to the Jewish excellence in music, physics and mathematics, whose languages are international and codes of pure denotation.

The European Jew did not want to remain a guest. He strove, as he has done in America, to take root. He gave strenuous, even macabre proof of his loyalty. In 1933-4, Jewish veterans of the First World War assured Herr Hitler of their patriotism, of their devotion to the German ideal. Shortly thereafter, even the limbless and the decorated were hauled to the camps. In 1940, when Vichy stripped French Jews of their rights, veterans of Verdun, holders of the *Médaille militaire*, men whose families had lived in France since the early nineteenth century, found themselves harried and stateless. In the Soviet Union a Jew is so designated on his identity card. Is it foolish or hysterical to suppose that, labour as he may, the Jew in a gentile nation-state sits near the door? Where, inevitably, he arouses distrust.

From Dreyfus to Oppenheimer, every burst of nationalism, of patriotic hysteria, has focused suspicion on the Jew. Such statistics probably have no real meaning, but it may well be that the proportion of Jews actually implicated in ideological or scientific disloyalty has been high. Perhaps because they have been vulnerable to blackmail and clandestine menace, because they are natural middlemen with an ancient ease in the export and import of ideas. But more essentially, I imagine, because they are pariahs whose sense of nationality has been made critical and unsteady. To a man who may tomorrow be in desperate flight across his own border, whose graveyard may be ploughed up and strewn with garbage, the nation-state is an ambiguous haven. Citizenship becomes not an inalienable right, a sacrament of *Blut und Boden*, but a contract which he must re-negotiate, warily, with each host.

The rootlessness of the Jew, the 'cosmopolitanism' denounced by Hitler, by Stalin, by Mosley, by every right-wing hooligan, is historically an enforced condition. The Jew finds no comfort in 'squatting on the window sill' (T. S. Eliot's courteous phrase). He would rather have been *echt Deutsch* or *Français de vieille souche* or Minuteman born, than 'Chicago Semite Viennese'. At most times he has been given no choice. But though uncomfortable in the extreme, his condition is, if we accept it, not without a larger meaning.

Nationalism is the venom of our age. It has brought Europe to the edge of ruin. It drives the new states of Asia and Africa like crazed lemmings. By proclaiming himself a Ghanaian, a Nicaraguan, a Maltese, a man spares himself vexation. He need not ravel out what he is, where his humanity lies. He becomes one of an armed, coherent pack. Every mob impulse in modern politics, every totalitarian design, feeds on nationalism, on the drug of hatred which makes human beings bare their teeth across a wall, across ten yards of waste ground. Even if it be against his harried will, his weariness, the Jew — or some Jews, at least — may have an exemplary role. *To show that whereas trees have roots, men have legs and are each other's guests.* If the potential of civilisation is not to be destroyed, we shall have to develop more complex, more provisional loyalties. There are, as Socrates taught, necessary treasons to make the city freer and more open to man. Even a Great Society is a bounded, transient thing compared to the free play of the mind and the anarchic discipline of its dreams.

When a Jew opposes the parochial ferocity into which nationalism so easily (inevitably) degenerates, he is paying an old debt. By one of the cruel, deep ironies of history, the concept of a chosen people, of a nation exalted above others by particular destiny, was born in Israel. In the vocabulary of Nazism there were elements of a vengeful parody on the Judaic claim. The theological motif of a people elected at Sinai is echoed in the pretence of the master race and its chiliastic dominion. Thus there was in the obsessed relation of Nazi to Jew a minute but fearful grain of logic.

But if the poison is, in ancient part, Jewish, so perhaps is the antidote, the radical humanism which sees man on the road to becoming man. This is where Marx is most profoundly a Jew (while at the same time arguing the dissolution of Jewish identity). He believed that class and economic status knew no frontiers, that misery had a common citizenship. He postulated that the revolutionary process would abolish national distinctions and antagonisms as industrial technology had all but eroded regional autonomy. The entire socialist utopia and dialectic of history is based on an international premise.

Marx was wrong; here, as in other respects, he thought too romantically, too well of men. Nationalism has been a major cause and beneficiary of two world wars. The workers of the world did not unite; they tore at each other's throats. Even beggars wrap themselves in flags. It was Russian patriotism, the outrage of national consciousness, not the vision of socialism and class solidarity, which enabled the Soviet Union to survive in 1941. In Eastern Europe, state socialism has left national rivalries fierce and archaic. A thousand miles of empty Siberian Steppe may come to matter more to Russia and China than the entire fabric of communist fraternity.

But though Marx was wrong, though the ideal of a non-national society seems mockingly remote, there is in the last analysis no other alternative to self-destruction. The earth grows too crowded, too harassed by the shadow of famine, to waste soil on barbed wire. Where he can survive as guest, where he can re-examine the relations between conscience and commitment, making his exercise of national loyalty scrupulous but also sceptical and humane, the Jew

can act as a valuable irritant. The chauvinist will snarl at his heels. But it is in the nature of a chase that those who are hunted are in advance of the pack.

That is why I have not, up till now, been able to accept the notion of going to live in Israel. The State of Israel is, in one sense, a sad miracle. Herzl's Zionist programme bore the obvious marks of the rising nationalism of the late nineteenth century. Sprung of inhumanity and the imminence of massacre, Israel has had to make itself a closed fist. No one is more tense with national feeling than an Israeli. He must be if his strip of home is to survive the wolf-pack at its doors. Chauvinism is almost the requisite condition of life. But although the strength of Israel reaches deep into the awareness of every Jew, though the survival of the Jewish people may depend on it, the nation-state bristling with arms is a bitter relic, an absurdity in the century of crowded men. And it is alien to some of the most radical, most humane elements in the Jewish spirit.

So a few may want to stay in the cold, outside the sanctuary of nationalism – even though it is, at last, their own. A man need not be buried in Israel. Highgate or Golders Green or the wind will do.

If my children should happen to read this one day, and if luck has held, it may seem as remote to them as it will to a good many of my contemporaries. If things go awry, it may help remind them that somewhere stupidity and barbarism have already chosen them for a target. This is their inheritance. More ancient, more inalienable than any patent of nobility.

George Steiner was born in Paris in 1929 and educated at the Universities of Chicago, Harvard and Oxford. Extraordinary Fellow of Churchill College, Cambridge and Professor of English and Comparative Literature at the University of Geneva, he is also currently Weidenfeld Visiting Professor of Comparative Literature at Oxford University. His many books include *The Death of Tragedy* (1961), *In Bluebeard's Castle* (1971), *After Babel* (1975), *Language and Silence* (1979) and the novel *The Portage to San Cristobal of A.H.* (1979).

Map showing the main
deportation railways to
Auschwitz. From
Martin Gilbert, *Atlas of
the Holocaust*,
Routledge, London
1993

Ronnie S. Landau

The Nazi Holocaust: Its Moral, Historical and Educational Significance

The Holocaust as an Educational Theme

The Nazi Holocaust is increasingly regarded as one of the most momentous events of modern history, if not of all time. No longer dismissed as a tragic by-product of the Second World War, nor explained away by a whole variety of simplistic, monolithic theories, the Holocaust has become a central reference point for humanity as it stands on the threshold of a new millennium.

The world of scholarship – like virtually every other section of society – at first received the Holocaust in stunned and awed silence: for almost two decades philosophers, educationalists, historians, psychologists and theologians could find precious little to say. Since the 1960s, however, the subject has generated a colossal body of literature. The awe is still there, but no longer the silence.

The Holocaust as a theme, both in popular contemporary culture and in more academic settings, has proved a most powerful, highly charged and malleable subject: at its most inspiring, capable of being mediated in ways that are spiritually enriching and morally uplifting; but in the hands of the irresponsible, ideologically motivated or malevolent, easily abused, politicised and misrepresented.

One trend that is slowly changing is the overwhelming preponderance, in the fields of Holocaust scholarship and literature, of those who are themselves Jewish. Forty years after the war it was estimated that well over ninety per cent of all the books written on the subject were composed by those who were either survivor-victims or who had some sense of belonging to the 'victim group' – ethnic, cultural or psychological. While it is, of course, understandable that this event should exert such a profound fascination for the Jewish people, there has unquestionably been a viciously circular tendency in the world of academe for the Holocaust to be labelled as a 'Jewish' discipline, thus discouraging and exempting many of those outside the victim group from trespassing on such 'sacred' territory.

What sense, if any, have the analytical approaches of philosophy, psychology, history, and political science made of this catastrophe? And – to address that critical question: is the Holocaust an utterly singular historical phenomenon, or is it in any way comparable to other examples of 'genocide'?

Certainly, much of the literature on the Holocaust is dominated by – I might almost say fixated on – this question of uniqueness versus universality – at times unhelpfully and frustratingly so. It is almost as though some historians of the Holocaust have felt obliged to adopt a pleading tone – 'please believe me, our "genocide" was utterly without parallel' – in order to obtain recognition of its significance. (And so often this approach, notwithstanding its inherent truth, can prove educationally counter-productive.) It could, indeed, be argued that 'recognition', to the extent that it now exists, has come about precisely because others have made a whole series of connections (at times, it must be said, superficially) between the Holocaust and other peoples' experiences, between Nazi motives and the intentions of other perpetrators and abusers of power, rather than by being particularly impressed by its absolute isolation from everything else in life ... and death.

When assessing the importance of the Holocaust, its uniqueness and universality should not be seen as mutually exclusive categories; but, on the contrary, as complementary and effective ways of grappling with the Holocaust and its lessons for us all. We must confront our past, not run away from it, or elevate it to a mysterious plane that is utterly beyond our grasp – the more so when its messages are so difficult and disturbing.

Without losing sight of the terrible uniqueness of the Holocaust as an historical phenomenon, it is educationally essential and therefore, I believe, legitimate to break it down into a range of specific human experiences, motives, crises and responses, with which it might be easier to identify and which can stand comparison with other predicaments.

This article includes material excerpted and adapted from the author's book The Nazi Holocaust *(I. B. Tauris, London, 1992)*

For example, German anti-Jewish legislation of 1933-8 can be related to attempts by other societies to marginalise certain groups by process of law – for instance the operation of Apartheid in South Africa (not in itself a genocidal situation but perhaps potentially so). The utter irrationality of the annihilation of Jews, inspired by the imagined threat they posed to German civilisation, carries echoes of the Armenian genocide at the hands of the Turks during the First World War. The isolation of the Jewish victims can, to some degree, be compared with that of the victims of the Cambodian massacre in the late 1970s. The self-righteousness of many of the Nazi perpetrators – the prevailing belief in the correctness and 'holiness' of their bloodthirsty undertaking – can be related to almost every massacre in human history which has been carried out in the name of a religious or imperial mission. These partial analogies are not, of course, exact, but they should be explored; superficial comparisons are as undesirable as the refusal to allow any comparison.

We should start – and for some this is a painful process – to see the Holocaust as more than a symbol of Jewish fate, Jewish unity and the need for Jewish survival. It is all of these, but it is also a major challenge to assumptions about 'progress' and 'civilisation'. The Holocaust shattered Western liberal dreams of reason and culture as forces which necessarily humanise us and which promote genuine tolerance of difference. It also destroyed, once and for all, the tottering belief that science and technology were securely harnessed for the good of humanity, as scientists, politicians, bureaucrats and generals found the means progressively to give destructive expression to their decisions and fantasies. The gradual 'bureaucratisation' of killing, exemplified above all by the Holocaust, has placed a dangerous and steadily increasing distance between the perpetrators and the consequences of their decisions and actions.

As several educationalists and philosophers have pointed out, the Holocaust can also be interpreted as a metaphor for the darker side of contemporary existence. It was, in part, the outcome of problems of identity – the alienation and isolation of the individual in our modern mass societies. Nazism appealed to people's need for a sense of belonging, loyalty and community which had been left dangerously unfulfilled by the modern, centralised state. It encouraged a state of mind whereby the individual could easily be sucked into the entire bureaucratic process. Bureaucracy is a human invention which can subjugate its inventor, undermine human conscience and allow individuals to abdicate personal moral responsibility by blindly obeying orders. In the words of C. P. Snow: 'When you look at the long and gloomy history of man you will find more hideous crimes have been committed in the name of obedience than have ever been committed in the name of rebellion'. (C. P. Snow, 'Either-Or', *Progressive*, February 1961, p.24.)

The importance of the Holocaust should not be sought in the specific and horrific details of its execution – sadly, mass brutality and slaughter are far from new in human history – nor in the behaviour, psychology, religion or ethics of the Jews who were its primary victims. Its uniqueness, in fact, has disconcertingly little to do with the harrowing experiences of individual victims. Instead, it lies in the *intentions* of its perpetrators and in the fact that these intentions were, for the most part, translated into reality – for the Jews were the only group marked out for total European annihilation, even in neutral countries and those not yet conquered. And this can, and must, be stated without diminishing in any way the suffering of any other group.

The uniqueness of the Holocaust also lies in the unprecedented way that the full might of a twentieth-century, industrially advanced State could be perverted, subordinated to a philosophy of destruction and then directed against a vulnerable, conspicuous, powerless and largely unresisting target.

The Holocaust was a totality – a global event. It was certainly made up of the sum of countless individual stories, attitudes, reactions and dilemmas; but it is also much more than the sum of those parts and cannot be adequately perceived through the prism of any one component part. The Holocaust had no precedent and, as an historical phenomenon, resists satisfactory explanation. It was, of course, a Jewish tragedy, but it was not only a Jewish tragedy; it also belongs to world history and to the realm of general humanities and moral studies. Jews, as the special victims of this unique event, are not the only potential victims of such man-made catastrophes, and their wretched experience has implications that go far beyond the Jewish world – implications of profound concern to the general historian, psychologist, theologian and educationalist.

In the hands of a few malevolent individuals, the subject of the Holocaust has been drawn into the spotlight purely so that it can be manipulated and denied. Far from constituting a serious analysis of the Holocaust, such 'revisionist' history serves more as an example of the kind of twisted thinking that actually contributed to the Nazi horrors in the first place. Of such 'historians', Michael Marrus has written with justifiable contempt in the preface of his excellent work, *The Holocaust in History* (1987): 'I see no reason why such people should set the agenda for the subject, any more than flat-earth theorists should set the agenda for astronomers'!

Jewish history in general and the Holocaust in particular must be taught in order to combat racial prejudice and the abuse of power. To fulfil this goal, the Holocaust should not be torn – as so regularly happens – from its historical and wider educational contexts. If the study of the Holocaust is cordoned off from other disciplines, divorced from other people's experiences, it will become inaccessible – an impossibly grim and remote area of study enacted in an educationally meaningless vacuum.

An enlightened and effective approach to communicating the Holocaust can be built on the following philosophical and educational premises which can be adapted to most pedagogical settings:

(1) The Holocaust was an event which was *both* unique *and* universal, of far-reaching significance for the Jewish people but also with momentous implications for everyone.

(2) If taught skilfully and responsibly, the study of the Holocaust can help socialise and even 'civilise'. It can serve as a highly effective educational tool for making students sensitive to the distinct problem of anti-Semitism; to the universal issues of minority status and minority identity; to the need most of us have for cultural and national pride; and to the dangers of racial and religious stereotyping, prejudice and hatred. But if taught badly, it can titillate, traumatise, mythologise and encourage a purely negative view of all Jewish history, of Jewish people and, indeed, of all victim groups.

(3) The Holocaust and its lessons should be considered within the following contexts simultaneously:
(a) that of Jewish history and the history of anti-Semitism;
(b) that of modern German history;
(c) that of 'genocide' in the nineteenth and twentieth centuries;
(d) that of the misuse of technology and bureaucracy in the twentieth century;
(e) that of the psychology of human prejudice and racism.

(4) Teacher and student alike must acknowledge that we all bring to bear on the study of the Holocaust our own changing experience, values and awareness and, inescapably, those of the society and the times in which we live.

(5) No one incident or experience can adequately convey the totality and magnitude of the Holocaust. This catastrophe comprised all kinds of elements, each adding a horrifying dimension to the whole. Neither Kovno, nor Treblinka, nor Wannsee nor Babi Yar can

alone represent the others. Collectively, however, they express the very worst that human beings can do to each other and to themselves.

The Central Role of Questions

The attempt to communicate and transmit this historical event is a task shot through with difficulties. Despite whole libraries devoted to it – at times to the point of 'information overload' – there is still no sure agreement on certain central issues. No adequate or simple explanation is possible or indeed desirable. Rather, we should try to identify the right questions and then work towards the possible answers and lessons to be inferred.

This is easier said than done – particularly in a scholastic environment, where clear answers are commonly expected from those entrusted with the task of education. At an early stage, the student of the Holocaust must try to rise above the need to stick explanatory labels on everything, and to resist the compulsion to reach precise, unequivocal conclusions in answer to the 'big' questions.

Such key questions would include the following:

(1) How, why and when did the Nazis determine a policy of total annihilation of the Jews of Europe?

(2) To what extent was the ferocity of the Nazi onslaught rooted in the peculiar social, economic and psychological circumstances prevailing in Germany in the years following her traumatic defeat in the First World War and the humiliating Treaty of Versailles?

(3) Can Germany's descent to barbarism be attributed, to any degree, to a fear of Bolshevism?

(4) Is it true that full-blooded Nazi anti-Jewishness had only a very marginal appeal to ordinary Germans, even among those who voted for Hitler?

(5) Why did a higher proportion of Jews survive in Fascist Italy and in countries allied to Germany, such as Rumania and Hungary, than in anti-Nazi Holland with its democratic tradition and long history of toleration towards Jews? Why did so many Jews die in Poland? Does the explanation lie in the religious anti-Semitism of the indigenous population? Or is the answer much more complex?

(6) How was it possible for such a supposedly 'civilised' society, which had given us Goethe, Beethoven and Brahms, to produce such barbarity, albeit of a largely dispassionate and coolly executed kind?

(7) How are we to assess the role of the Reich railway officials who drew up rail schedules and even charged 'package tour' fares to unwitting passengers who were then transported in cattle trucks to extermination camps in the East?

(8) How was it possible for certain individuals, whose role would prove indispensable to the carrying out of the 'Final Solution of the Jewish Question', to be subtly conditioned into believing that to kill Jews was morally no worse than to brush dandruff off their jackets – and, on the contrary, was a morally good thing?

(9) Why do the Jews *appear* to have offered so little resistance everywhere? (Do we even have the right to ask this question?)

(10) How can we begin to evaluate the degree of moral responsibility of the Jewish leaders and the specially established Jewish police force in the ghettos of Poland?

(11) How are we to judge the behaviour and responsibility of numerous other groups: ordinary Germans; the citizens of defeated and occupied countries; Germany's allies, such as Italy and Hungary; the various churches throughout Europe; the anti-Nazi Allies, in particular Great Britain, the United States and the Soviet Union; neutral governments, like those of Sweden, Switzerland, Spain and Eire; and, finally, the Jews themselves?

(12) How big a factor is the astonishing human capacity for indifference to the plight of others (present in all societies and arguably on the increase) in explaining the path to Auschwitz and Treblinka?

(13) What does the methodical slaughter of one-and-a-half million Jewish children say about the presence or interest of (a) God in human affairs?

(14) What is the relationship between Nazi anti-Jewish ideology and earlier expressions of anti-Judaism and anti-Semitism in European history?

(15) What was the difference between the Jewish experience of Nazism and that of the five-and-a-half million other civilians – Gypsies, Poles, Russians, homosexuals, Jehovah's Witnesses, communists, socialists and others – who were also murdered in cold blood? In other words, why does the term 'Holocaust' strictly refer to the Jewish experience alone?

(16) And, finally, a question that dominates Holocaust literature: is the catastrophe that overwhelmed the Jews of Europe an utterly unique historical phenomenon, or is it a case within the category of 'genocide'?

An emotional and intellectual helplessness in the face of the enormity of the Holocaust has led many representatives of the 'victim group', understandably perhaps, to seek to monopolise the event and to be disinclined to 'share' it with others. What has sometimes followed – and this is deeply regrettable, and invariably has the unhelpful effect of alienating those outside the victim group – is a grotesque competition in suffering.

The Holocaust has proved so incomprehensible that it has sometimes led to what has been called the 'demonisation' of Hitler, Nazism and the crime itself. This is, of course, similar to the medieval Christian view of the Devil as the source of all evil – an entity which remains outside human perception and grasp. Such demonisation leads to an obsession with evil as a purely external force, preventing us from searching for it inside ourselves and, most significantly, within the societies, technological systems and bureaucratic structures we have created.

If there are any lessons to be derived from the Holocaust, there is no sense whatever in ascribing its execution to Satanic monsters: for then it becomes unrelated to what is humanly intelligible. What is more, such a reading of Nazism would involve an abstract dehumanisation of Nazis – and often indiscriminately of all Germans – which was precisely the Nazi attitude towards Jews.

On the contrary, we must understand that the Holocaust, for all its freakishness, was a human event – all too human – which shows that humanity is, on the one hand, eminently capable of doing anything that our technology makes possible, horrifyingly ready to perform unimagined acts of wholesale destruction and self-destruction. The Holocaust, to paraphrase Samuel Pisar, a survivor of Auschwitz, was not, as he thought at the time, the end of the world, but possibly the beginning of the end of the world, if we ignore its universal implications.

Humankind is also, the Holocaust shows us, alarmingly prone – especially in the twentieth century – to replacing personal ethical standards with collective ones that appear to exempt the individual from accountability. However, the Holocaust also provides evidence that the best is also in us – for some, in their exercise of moral choice, chose good against the polluted stream.

Postwar Genocide and The International Community: The Lessons of the Holocaust Unheeded?

The Holocaust occurred before many of us were born, and perhaps we have been tempted, when contemplating this event, to pass judgement on the 'passive' behaviour of our parents' and grandparents' generation. Yet, within the past few years, while most of us sat idly by, many hundreds of thousands of civilians in the former Yugoslavia – in a European country where many of us had our vacations booked only a few short summers ago – have had their civil, national and human rights trampled under foot, have been forcibly displaced and, in countless cases, raped, tortured and murdered. Our governments and other agencies failed utterly to make an effective intervention until it was too late. What was essentially a savage war of national aggression and 'genocide' was dignified and softened by the term 'civil war', an appellation intended to excuse our inaction – to the everlasting shame of our political leaders and of ourselves.

That an international war crimes tribunal has been established to investigate and bring to justice those held responsible for 'war crimes' and 'crimes against humanity' in the former Yugoslavia is certainly welcome. It may even prove to have far-reaching implications for the future, especially the future safety of minority groups. But if it is to have the desired preventive and educational effect, it would be as well to examine the mistakes of the past forty-five years: in particular, the consistent unwillingness and apparent inability of the member-states of the United Nations to intervene in the 'sovereign affairs' of one of their own number; and their consequent failure to invoke, even once, the United Nations Genocide Convention of 1948. For man-made catastrophes since the Second World War have by no means been limited – despite the previous experience of the Nazi Holocaust – to horrendous events in European Bosnia.

The international community's attitude to genocide during the past half-century is instructive and cautionary. Although the incidence of genocide or near-genocide has been a depressingly constant feature of recorded history, it was events in Nazi-occupied Europe in 1943 that prompted the international jurist, Raphael Lemkin, to invent the term 'genocide'; this was, of course, before anyone had a full appreciation of the enormity of what had occurred in the annihilation factories in Poland. Significantly, Lemkin was concerned not merely with punishing perpetrators of actual crimes against civilian populations, but with anticipating and warding off potential atrocities, massacres and genocidal onslaughts.

According to the 1948 Genocide Convention, perpetrators were to be held accountable whether they were legitimate rulers, public officials or private individuals. They were to be tried either by a competent tribunal of the state in which the acts were perpetrated, or by an international penal tribunal whose jurisdiction had been accepted by the members of the UN.

However, as if in anticipation of the later reluctance to apply its sanctions, the convention was weakened by a number of member-states who insisted on emasculating its terms of reference. Prominent in this respect was the Soviet Union, which asserted that genocide, as committed by the Nazis, was bound up with a decaying phase of imperialism, the implication being that the convention would be unlikely to have any future application. Moreover, within the Soviet bloc, the specificity of the crime against the Jews came to be subsumed under the general heading of Fascist crimes against the peoples of Eastern Europe.

Perhaps it was felt that a full definition, enshrined in international law, would in some way encroach upon and threaten the sovereignty of independent states – the very bodies most capable of committing the crime in question.

What is beyond dispute, however, is that despite the terrifying and well-documented precedent of the Nazi Holocaust and despite the adoption of this convention by the United Nations, genocide has continued to disfigure human existence on this planet.

One of the hallmarks of genocide has consistently been the international community's inaction until it is too late. In this sense, the United Nations's Genocide Convention has in practice been a dead letter. The failure of the United Nations to invoke the Genocide Convention in the case of Cambodia, for instance, and, what is more, the alleged participation of 'representatives' of Pol Pot's Khmer Rouge in the United Nations' efforts to plan the future of Cambodia, has led to widespread condemnation, but solely at a popular level; only very rarely has it been voiced in governmental circles. It has consequently even been suggested in some quarters that the United Nations has somehow forfeited its right to be regarded as a serious bulwark against future genocides.

In the opinion of some, though certainly not all, commentators, victims of genocide in the post-Holocaust period would include the following groups: the Bengalis, 1971; the Hutu of Burundi, 1972; the Cambodians, 1975-9; the East Timor islanders, 1975-present; the Algerians, 1945-62; the Christian southern Sudanese, 1955-present; the Indonesian Communists, 1965-7; the Ibos (Biafra), 1966-70; the political opponents of the Pinochet regime in Chile, 1973; the Mayan Indians in Guatemala, 1980-present; the peoples of Tigray and Eritrea (Ethiopia), 1980-93; the Iraqi Kurds, 1988 and 1991; the Chittagong hill tribes in Pakistan (later Bangladesh), late 1940s-present; the Ache and other Amerindians in Brazil and Paraguay, 1960s-present; the Tibetans, 1959-present; the West Papuans, 1969-present; opponents of Stalinism in the USSR, up to 1953; the Ugandans (especially Ugandan Asians), 1972-85; the left-wing opponents of the Argentinian Junta, 1978-9; the Marsh Arabs of Southern Iraq, 1991-present; Muslims and Croats in the former Yugoslavia, 1992-present; and the Tutsi in Rwanda, 1994-present.

As we approach the new millennium, the argument still rages as to whether ageing Nazis – 'tired and broken old men' – should be put on trial for war crimes against humanity. The arguments in favour focus on the pursuit of justice rather than on vengeance, and on the moral and educational value of such trials. Opponents emphasise the 'near impossibility' of producing reliable witnesses to ensure fair trials so long after the event. They also draw attention to the inconsistency and selectiveness whereby Nazi 'criminals' are hunted down, while the perpetrators of other genocidal atrocities, for example Pol Pot, Saddam Hussein and their henchmen, go unpunished and, in the former's case, appear to enjoy the protection of powerful Western countries.

In effect, the Nuremburg War Crimes proceedings, important as they were both symbolically and in their establishment of international moral principles, did little more than pay lip service to the need to deal with the thousands who were guilty of monstrous crimes (as we now know, neither West nor East Germany was ever de-Nazified). Yet, for all their inadequacy, the Nuremberg trials were exceptional in having been held at all. For no international tribunals have since been convened, either to examine charges against alleged Nazi war criminals or to investigate other palpable examples of genocide.

The key issues, challenges and questions are these: can we contemplate a statute of limitations on the commission of genocidal and related crimes? Given that the victims were themselves given no second chance, can there be any moral, judicial, exemplary or rehabilitatory justification for letting mass murderers go free merely because of the passage of time? In any case, do later generations have the moral right to forgive or exonerate the perpetrators for their crimes? How can the international community show evenhandedness in its investigation of such monstrous crimes, and thus avoid the construction of a hierarchy of suffering which condemns some genocides to virtual oblivion, whereas others remain at the forefront of our consciousness? While preserving the distinctiveness and unique character of each genocide, are we prepared to make 'connections' between different genocides – ie identify common features – which may enable us to establish early warning systems to prevent the continuing abuse, persecution and destruction of groups, and the possible obliteration of cultures? Such links and points of resemblance might include: the psychological perspective and motivation of the perpetrator; the dehumanised image within a society of the victim or potential victim; the centrality of the State as a source of 'authority' for genocidal action; and the types of political context which appear to serve as the necessary catalyst (though not the explanation) of genocide: almost always a convulsive framework such as war, revolution, imperial expansion and, especially in the latter half of the twentieth century, the chaos resulting from decolonisation.

Should there now be a new code, based on the Geneva Convention, the United Nations Genocide Convention, or other agreed rules of International Law, and – most important – on what we have learned of the causes and nature of the Nazi Holocaust and of genocide during the decades since the Second World War? Is there a case for establishing an accountable international monitoring system, which can be supported, if necessary, by United Nations force? (In 1991, the anticipated genocide against the Kurds of northern Iraq was averted – or delayed – merely because of the fortuitous presence of hundreds of Western journalists in the wake of the Gulf War: Western leaders and the United Nations were literally shamed into taking temporary preventive action.) A related question concerns the possible establishment of a permanent multi-national War Crimes and Genocide Tribunal which might expose, try and punish those leaders and followers found guilty of violations of the new code.

The past few years have witnessed enormous upheavals and transformations, especially in Europe. Between 1945 and 1990, Europe remained essentially unchanged, as did the balance of international power. The postwar geopolitical arrangements were born largely out of conditions emerging from the defeat of Nazism. Consequently, there has been, within our culture and society, an organic link to the Nazi period, kept alive by memories and memorabilia (films, books and the like). The new world order and the passing of generations have inevitably dimmed memories. They may also dim the sense of horror and revulsion which, in the industrialised world at least, had (before the war in Bosnia) served to stem any tendencies for repetition. Should there be any truth in the propositions that forgetting is repeating and that failure to understand is to condone, the purpose of this volume and of the exhibition it accompanies is to make a contribution in helping us both to remember and to try to understand.

Ronnie S. Landau is the former Educational Director of the Spiro Institute for the Study of Jewish History and Culture. Founding Director of the British Holocaust Educational Project, he writes widely on modern Jewish history and the Holocaust. He is the author of *The Nazi Holocaust* (1992).

Ziva Amishai-Maisels

The Complexities of Witnessing

Reproduced from Holocaust and Genocide Studies, *Vol.2, No.1, 1987, pp.123-47*

How did witnesses depict the Holocaust in art? What scenes did they select? The answer seems at first to be simple: they covered all aspects of the Holocaust to such an extent that, arranged in their proper order, these art works could be used to make a detailed documentary movie on the subject, replacing film-clips and photographs.[1] In fact, despite the vast amount of photographic material that exists on the Holocaust, many drawings and paintings depict otherwise unrecorded scenes.[2] However, on analysis, this answer turns out to be simplistic. Although, taking all the works together, every aspect was covered, different artists chose different subjects. Furthermore, the artist's experience of the Holocaust and the aims of his art not only determined his choice of material, but its treatment.

Much has been written recently about the reasons inmates created art in the camps and ghettos under almost impossible and often dangerous circumstances. The reasons usually cited fall roughly into five categories: official art; spiritual resistance through the assertion of individuality; the affirmation and commemoration of life; catharsis; and witnessing.[3] This paper will deal primarily with the problem raised by the last category, which is perhaps the most widespread of them all.

Being a witness is not as simple as it sounds: the artist must choose not only *what* to depict, but *how* to depict it. Here the problem of style enters the arena: is he to be a 'camera' – an objective realist portraying every detail? Or is he to be an Expressionist, heightening reality with his own subjective feelings in order to convey not only what life in the camp *looked* like, but also what it *felt* like, and thus to make the spectator respond emotionally with pity, identification or revulsion? That such a choice was available to the camp artist emerges from the fact that many of them were not novices, but had either studied art or worked as artists before their incarceration, and thus had a fair knowledge of past and contemporary art and of the range of styles and iconographical schemes open to them.[4]

Most artists, whatever their previous style had been, opted for naturalistic descriptions of camp life. However, even this situation is not clear-cut: there are differences in style not only between different artists, but even between an individual artist's treatment of different themes. For instance, many of Boris Taslitzky's linear sketches of Buchenwald depict scenes which could be taking place anywhere (Fig.1).

Fig.1 Boris Taslitzky, *Along the Barbed Wire,* *c.*1943 - 4, pencil on paper. From Boris Taslitzky, *111 Dessins faits à Buchenwald* (Bibliothèque Française, Paris, 1945), No.25

His figures often have sad expressions, but they seem to be simply hanging around and chatting while they wait for food. They talk to other inmates through the barbed-wire fence or lean nonchalantly against it. In another sketch, two men sit quietly talking, remembering Paris, in a scene which could have been drawn at a Paris café, while his depiction of the official camp orchestra portrays men who could be playing anywhere. These drawings, done in a light, sketchy style, exhibit the external appearance of the camp without distorting it. He did not beautify the scenes – he simply chose scenes of daily life that look almost normal. In fact, this choice was forced on him by his role as eye-witness: he chose moments when he himself could rest and draw what he saw around him, something he could not do, for instance, during a work detail. There is a major difference, however, between these works and photographs of the camps. Instead of portraying the masses seen in many camp photographs, Taslitzky, like most camp artists, focused on a relatively small number of people, both as a means of preserving his own and the other inmates' individuality against the Nazis' attempt to dehumanise them, and as a way of dealing with the subject in terms which could be grasped by artist and spectator alike.[5]

Although Taslitzky used the same naturalistic, objective style in depicting more horrifying subjects, such as *Block 51 and Block of Human 'Guinea Pigs'* or the skeletal figure of *Prof. Halbwachs Enduring Medical Care a Few Days Before his Death*, an element of Expressionism creeps into the shocked faces of the *New Arrivals Regarding a Corpse Carried by Them* (Fig.2), completely distorting the face of one of them and turning him into a living corpse. This tendency to Expressionism is further heightened in his numerous renderings of death and corpses.[6] This difference in style derives from a clear artistic choice to heighten the communicative power of scenes of death, as well as from an unconscious reaction: one can remain relatively objective about a line of people waiting for soup, but death, especially in Holocaust terms, evokes both anger and a strong subjective response which surfaces in art as Expressionism.

Henri Pieck, on the other hand, preferred a heightened realism combined with a choice of dramatic subjects in his depictions of Buchenwald. His realistically drawn skeletal figures are carried by friends: some barely manage to sit up; others collapse and die while waiting for the doctor. To underline the physiognomic differences between Jewish and Russian prisoners, he exaggerated their facial features. Occasionally, however, his exaggerations verge on caricature, as he tried to express grotesque situations, such as the Dutch prisoner who gloats over his booty of potato-peelings, or the French inmate smoking a cigarette butt beside unburied corpses, while others fight over barrel-scrapings in the background. Here again the artist chose his style to suit his material, treating it subjectively in order to clarify his message to the spectator.[7]

Pieck's most striking works are his most realistic ones, where he combines grim details, down to his model's missing teeth, with the strong expression on their faces and gestures, as they labour or stand behind barbed wire peering out at the spectator (Fig.3).[8] His realism is, however, different from that found in photographs of the camps. For instance, after the liberation, Margaret Bourke-White visited Buchenwald and photographed the inmates standing quietly, resigned and almost apathetic behind barbed wire as they confront the spectator, crowding close to the fence to get into the photograph (Fig.4).[9] Each has a slightly different expression on his face, as he

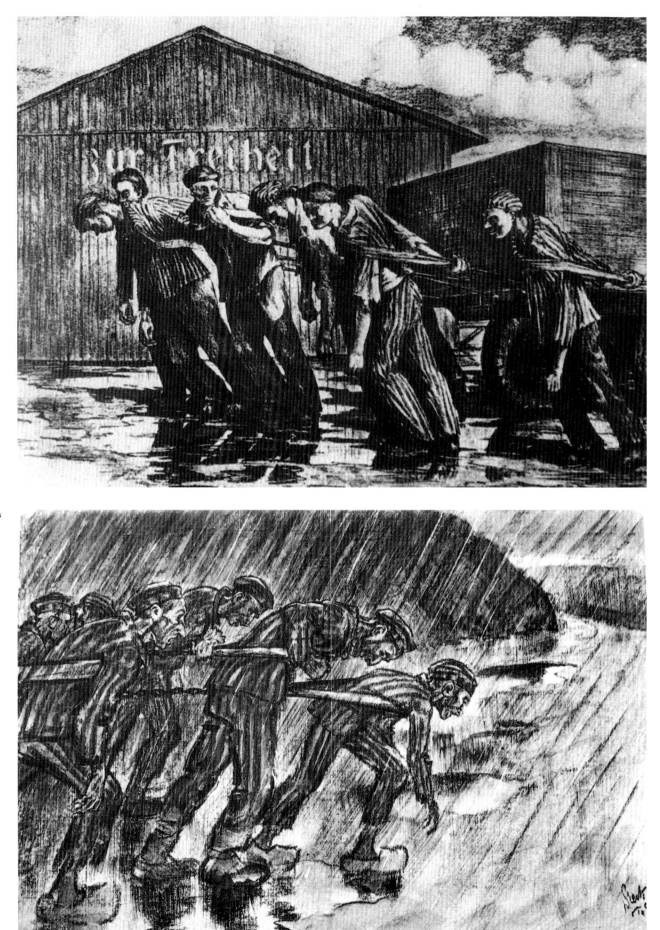

Fig.5 Odd Nansen, *Lorry Fatigue Party*, 1944, pen and ink

Fig.6 Henri Pieck, *Jews Before the Car*, 1945. From Henri Pieck, *Buchenwald*, pp.6 - 7

Fig.7 Maurycy
Bromberg, <i>Five Jews in
One Yoke</i>, undated,
charcoal, 38 × 28 cm

responds as an individual to the new situation.
Bourke-White has captured their emaciated physical
condition as well as their feelings of anxiety, doubt
and hope. Pieck depicted the same physical condition,
but emphasised it by removing the caps of the two
men on the left to reveal their shaven heads. By using
a 'close-up', and only hinting at other inmates in the
background, Pieck heightens our awareness both of
the barbed-wire fence and of the feelings of the
inmates. He enlarges the shiny barbs slightly so that
they appear more ominous, and has the prisoners, no
longer apathetic, surge forward against the barbed
wire in a movement which suggests their desire to
break out of the camp. The two on the left rejoice at
their liberation, their expressions in marked contrast
to that of the man in the centre, who stares dully
ahead, and to the half-crazed look of the Frenchman
on the right. This last can be interpreted either as
connoting deep suffering or as the threatening glare of
a man bent on revenge. The emotions Pieck expressed
here are stronger and more dramatic than those in the
photograph. The artist exposed the powerful inner

feelings of his fellow inmates, while the camera captured the blander face they had learned to turn
towards the world in order to survive.

The problem facing the prisoner-artist was thus
how to reveal feelings as well as facts so that the spectator would grasp the truth about the camps. The
solutions involved iconographic and stylistic choices
which can best be studied by analysing two subjects
involving daily life in the camp as they were depicted
by various artists under the same or different conditions.

The first subject we will investigate – camp labour –
raises some of the problems that confronted the artist
interested in creating a convincing witness report. A
favourite theme involved men pulling huge rollers or
wagons, to which they are hitched like animals. Odd
Nansen's realistic drawing of inmates yoked to a truck
which they pull with all their might through the mud,
done at Sachsenhausen in 1944 (Fig.5), puts the
emphasis on the difficulty of the labour rather than on
the individual character of the prisoners. His depiction closely resembles photographs of this scene, but

Fig.8 Ilya Repin, *Volga Boatmen*, c.1872, oil on canvas, 1.32 × 2.81 m

he added a touch of bitter sarcasm by means of the inscription on the barracks, 'To Freedom', commenting through this combination of image and words on the Nazi slogan 'Arbeit Macht Frei'.[10] Henri Pieck depicted the same scene at Buchenwald in 1945 (Fig.6), but heightened the picture's expressiveness and emotional impact. He added rain to the mud, and his yoked Jews pull with the last bit of their strength at a weight too heavy for them to move – a weight which is all the heavier as it exists only in the spectator's mind: it does not appear in the picture. He concentrated on the effort which doubles the lead figure over, and the physical strain visible in the prisoners' gestures and in the slightly exaggerated physiognomy of their faces, their mouths open as they gasp for breath.[11]

This type of compositional choice and exaggeration is also found in Maurycy Bromberg's Expressionist *Five Jews in One Yoke* (Fig.7) executed at Auschwitz.[12]

Instead of individuals, he portrayed shaven-headed 'skeletons' whose striped uniforms blend into a single mass. Rather than pulling the roller horizontally or diagonally out of the picture so that all the details will be clear, they lean towards us, sharply foreshortened, focusing our attention on their efforts to pull the weight behind them and on the misery and resignation in their faces.

These three compositions, for all their accurate reportage, have something very surprising in common. They are all based on well-known Russian prototypes with which the artists were clearly familiar. Nansen's composition, the poses of some of his figures, and even the type of yoke used, are based on his memories of Ilya Repin's *Volga Boatmen* of c.1872 (Fig.8). Nansen simply added the camp barracks and uniform, and converted the boat into a heavy wagon.[13] Pieck, using the same prototype, went beyond Repin and Nansen in expression: his labourers are even more exhausted,

31

Fig.9 Ilya Repin, *Volga Boatmen*, c.1872, oil on canvas, 62 × 97 cm

and the object being towed, which Repin barely indicated at the far right, is now totally excluded. Neither artist 'remembered' the protesting youth in the centre of Repin's composition, who formed an important part of the Russian artist's social protest. What they wanted to portray here was not resistance but unmitigated and hopeless slavery.

Bromberg, on the other hand, adapts another version of Repin's painting (Fig.9), adjusting it to his conception of camp labour in another way. While preserving the composition as a whole and especially the positions of the figures, he stressed their misery by means of their bald, skull-like heads, and joined them into one anonymous mass by means of their striped uniforms. He further accentuated the danger their labour entailed by bringing the roller close up behind them – as opposed to Repin's distant ship – so that it becomes clear that one false move will cause them to perish under its weight.[14]

These comparisons raise important questions concerning camp art and the workings of the minds of the artists. On the one hand, they could declare truthfully that they were interested solely in producing witness reports, or as Karol Konieczny stated: 'My drawings ought not to be subjected to scrutiny and aesthetic artistic criticism; an aesthete will not find material in them for professional criticism. I wish them to be considered a living and shocking document of a world of horror and torment.'[15] On the other hand, Konieczny himself had studied art in Cracow for a year before his internment.[16] Thus in analysing inmate art, one must bear in mind that despite their conscious aims, the artists were not created in the camps, and that each of them brought with him his own cultural background, previous knowledge of and often even practice of art. Before ever they arrived in the camps, they had digested iconographical and stylistic traditions that would stand them in good stead when they sought to

Fig.10 Avigdor Arikha,
*Boyhood Deportation
Drawing: Another Work
Scene*, 1943, pencil on
paper

artists, to the point that very few are able to escape from their inculcated traditions and greet new experiences – including that of the Holocaust – with a *tabula rasa*. Visual associations such as those discussed above automatically creep in and transform the primary experience into a compound which includes conscious goals and artistic prototypes. This will especially be the case when such 'witness reports' were not sketched on the spot – which is the case with almost all depictions of camp labour – but in the secrecy of the barracks, where the memory of the actual scene would tend to blend more freely with that of the visual prototype.[17]

However, even when we can be fairly sure that such prototypes are lacking, it will still be clear that the artist made decisions to heighten the expressive power of his work, even though he may have done so subconsciously. This was the case with the drawings of a talented boy of fourteen who later became an artist, using the name Avigdor Arikha. In a drawing eventually captioned 'Those no longer able to work were in danger of selection and so hid their weakness as best they could' (Fig.10), the meaning is actually clear from the drawing itself. The elongated skeletal figure tottering under the burden of the stone he carries, must soon collapse and die, even without the help of the slave-master's stick raised to beat him (on the right). Arikha conveyed this impression by emphasising the physical distortions and the tilt of the body, and the shadow it casts on the ground. He claims that he made these seemingly mature artistic choices entirely unconsciously, and given his age at the time this is probably true. Yet he too did not do the drawing on the spot but shortly after seeing the scene, rearranging it subconsciously in his memory so that it would convey the message he later appended to it without the need of words.[18]

The second subject we will analyse here – living conditions in the notorious bunk-beds stacked one above the other, called 'boxes' – raises somewhat different questions, since many of the drawings to be dis-

Fig.11 Henri Pieck,
*Interior of a Hut in the
Little Camp*, c.1945.
From Henri Pieck,
Buchenwald, pp.10 - 11

maximise the expressive and communicative power of their 'witness reports'. This kind of background influences even photographers, consciously or unconsciously, dictating the subjects to be photographed and the angle from which the shot should be taken. It is an even more powerful formative force in the case of

cussed were done while the artist sat confronting the scene he described. Photographs of these bunks, taken for the most part after the liberation, show masses of figures packed into them with no place to move, their skull-like heads sticking out as though reaching for air.[19] Many of the inmates who depicted the 'boxes' made them seem more bearable, although they too showed heads or limbs protruding from the over-crowded quarters. Taslitzky and Pieck (Fig.11) drew figures both seated and standing in front of the bunks in Buchenwald, while other inmates are either lying or sitting on the bunks. Taslitzky did so in a naturalistic, sympathetic style, objectively reporting a fact. Pieck, as usual, intensified the scene by means of a height-ened realism, stressing the misery of the Russian pris-oners and the impossibly crowded conditions in the bunks.[20]

These typical views depict the 'boxes' from the out-side. However, in two of Taslitzky's sketches, done in the same naturalistic style, he portrayed the view from within. In one close-up, he crowded two figures into the upper bunk along with a sleeping man, and hinted at the lower tiers of beds by showing the head of another man asleep below. The second sketch (Fig.12) was drawn seated in the top tier, and shows a number of people sleeping beside and atop each other. At first glance, one notices two men in the centre, but soon we become aware of other figures to the right and left; finally a hand and foot set above the central heads attract our attention to two more figures in the background. By not depicting the bed itself, Taslitzky creates the feeling that beneath these figures lie still others and that they are piled high to the beams of the ceiling. He brings the spectator *into* the bunk-bed, making him experience the conditions there himself. However, if one is not familiar with the photographs or the other drawings in the series, one may not be able to understand exactly what is being portrayed.[21]

Other artists sought to arouse the spectator's sym-pathy by adding an indication of death. For instance, Henry Behr, working in Theresienstadt in 1944, wrote

Fig.12 Boris Taslitzky, *Sleeping in the 'Boxes'*, c.1943 - 4, pencil on paper. From Boris Taslitzky, *111 Dessins faits à Buchenwald*, No.35

Fig.13 Auguste Favier,
*Block in the Little
Camp*, 1943, ink

on the back of his picture: 'In the foreground a young
woman mourns her husband's death.' This explains
why she is clutching her head, and draws attention to
the figure covered with a sheet behind her, whose head
and feet protrude ever so slightly above the mattress.[22]
Arnold Daghani, on the other hand, in works done in
Transnistria in 1943, stressed the corpse being lowered
to the ground from the upper bunk in a composition
strongly reminiscent of the Deposition of Christ.[23]

Auguste Favier introduced the idea of death in a
different way. In a 1943 drawing from Buchenwald
(Fig.13), he retained the distant view of the 'boxes',
but stressed the skeletal quality of the inmates: the
bunks are filled with rows of skull-like heads, and two

of the figures leaving the 'boxes' are nude living car-
cases, one of whom has to be helped down by his com-
rades. This reduction to skin and bones is also stressed
on the right: behind a fairly healthy man in a camp
uniform, one semi-nude 'skeleton' supports another.
Here, the choice of subject – not life but a slow drain-
ing off of energy into death – led to the choice of
style: the elongated thin figures and the walking
'skeletons' give the scene a macabre quality not found
in the works discussed above. The other artists show
scenes that are crowded but livable. Here, we enter a
gruesome world which conveys perhaps more 'truth'
than the more 'realistic' depictions.[24]

Given these different modes of representation,

Taslitzky's change in attitude after the liberation is noteworthy. In *The Death of Danielle Casanova at Buchenwald* of 1950 (Fig.14),[25] he abandoned his calm, objective reportage for a dramatic subject and an Expressionist style. In the centre Danielle lies like a Christian martyr, dressed in white, with flowers in her hands. She is mourned frantically by the women around her, one of whom supports her while another kisses her feet in a symbolism evocative of the Pietà. To heighten the pathos, Taslitzky exaggerated the gestures, facial expressions and skeletal quality of the figures surrounding the 'saint': he opened their robes to reveal their distorted bodies, and emphasised their bony arms, one of which hangs down almost lifelessly

from the upper bunk. Even more surprising than this dramatic treatment is the style: the figures are elongated, angular, often flattened and always harsh, in marked contrast to his matter-of-fact rendering of camp scenes while he was a prisoner.

Taslitzky explained the painting's religious symbolism as well as its non-realistic style. After he had completed his large painting of Buchenwald,[26] his friend, Laurent Casanova, a leader of the French communist party and former Resistance fighter, proposed that he do something that would touch the hearts of French women, and he responded with a theme which symbolised for him the *true* nature of their struggle against Fascism and their martyrdom – the death of

Fig.14 Boris Taslitzky, *The Death of Danielle Casanova at Buchenwald*, 1950, oil on canvas, 2 × 3 m

another communist Resistance leader, Laurent's wife, Danielle, at Auschwitz on 9 May 1943. On the painting, he wrote a line from a poem by Louis Aragon: 'There will be flowers when you return', because

the subject of the picture is the theft from all of the Maries of France ... of the flowers that had been promised to them ... *The subject of the picture is my indignation*! ... The subject ... is the branch of *lilacs* set in Danielle's hands ... You know, flowers were forbidden in the camps. The women who worked outside the camps brought back, at the risk of being searched, under their clothes, this small branch of lilac to be placed in the hands of the dead Danielle ... [It] expresses the love of the women there for one whose death was not felt to be that of just anyone ... It was Danielle, the extraordinary helpmate, who would not know the liberation they knew was approaching; who had helped many to hold out till then, to survive ... [Her] memory remains a living example ... *My subject is a resurrection* ...

The scene that I represent was never susceptible to any photographic realism. Danielle did not die in the midst of her companions. It would have been treason, however, to paint her in solitude. The truth is the branch of lilac. *I did not make a historical reconstruction* ... Danielle is dressed in white ... Why? Traditionally, one gives the dress to virgins, to saints ... For Danielle, it was simply that being a dentist, she had the right to [wear] a white blouse. In that, pictorial traditions are superimposed on reality ... a new content is substituted for an ancient one ... one could say that the whole subject is religious.[27]

Taslitzky's explanation clarifies the reasons for his changes in style and subject-matter. In 1950, he was no longer recording scenes he saw before his eyes, but drawing on his memories to express the nightmare he had survived. Gone is the restraint; it has been replaced by a violent anger and aggressiveness that makes itself felt in both subject and style. No longer simply an eye-witness, he is now the prosecutor out to arouse his audience through full use of his emotive powers, in order to express truths which lie behind the visual facts.

An entirely different approach to an Expressionist rendering of the living conditions in the camps was taken by Bedrich Fritta at Theresienstadt. In one drawing (Fig.15), an emaciated man, his elongated body distorted and his head enlarged to stress his near skeletal condition, is portrayed within the confines of the barracks.[28] Although the components of the scene were also found in Favier's drawing, Fritta, as opposed to Favier, took distortion beyond exaggeration into the realm of the grotesque, and heightened his effect by his unsympathetic view of some of the figures in the background. In the lowest bunk on the right, a fat man gorges himself on food which he keeps hidden in a suitcase, while all that is visible of the figure in the upper bunk is a pair of legs and one big, undoubtedly smelly foot. The sharp perspective of the room heightens the feeling of a lack of normalcy in this hopeless situation.

Here, there is an element of self-criticism which arose from several causes, at least one of which involved the peculiar privileges of life at Theresienstadt. In another drawing, Fritta contrasts the 'luxurious' quarters and high life of a ghetto big-wig with the condition of the masses.[29] The former has a room to himself – albeit made of crates and a curtain – with furniture, flowers in a vase and paintings, one of which depicts an erotic scene. This painting on the wall suggests the relationship of the couple in the room who drink a toast and read poetry while reclining in easy chairs. They are shown in a caricatural style, which despite their emaciated bodies, can arouse only antagonism. Sympathy is reserved for the poor Jews huddled below. Although they are also treated in an Expressionist style which verges on caricature, emphasis is placed on their helplessness: the dying woman at the left will soon join the corpses which litter the foreground, among whom sit a wide-eyed emaciated child and old folk hunched over and withdrawn into themselves.[30] One young man looks upwards blindly towards the privileged pair. Beside him sits a man with a prominent Jewish star who clearly expresses the artist's feelings: looking with fury at the corpse in front of him, he seems to be brooding on a horrible revenge.

Anger, however, is not the only cause for this style

Fig.15 Bedrich Fritta, *Lodging in the Attic*, c.1943 - 4, ink and wash, 38 × 28 cm

Fig.16 Bedrich Fritta, *In the Attic*, *c.*1942 - 3, pen and ink and wash on paper, 55 × 84 cm

in Fritta's work; he undoubtedly first turned to it in an attempt to influence the spectator. *In the Attic* (Fig.16) does not contain bunk-beds, but it stresses the impossibly overcrowded conditions under which Jews were forced to live even in the model camp.[31] The accent is on the old and helpless, on people who have lost their will to live. Although most are sunk in deep apathy, some try to carry on normal functions, such as the women going to the bathroom and getting dressed at the right. Fritta's treatment of the scene enhances his message: large figures appear beside small ones, upside-down heads are set into odd corners; every space is filled in this topsy-turvy world in which all sense of proportion has been lost. Here, Expressionism has again been pushed to the level of

caricature and the grotesque, but there is no mockery: the spectator is asked to pity those living in these wretched conditions and to help them.

The result of these miserable conditions is brought out in Fritta's symbolic use of bunk-beds in *Quarters of the Aged* (Fig.17).[32] Here the bunks are set into a niche in the wall, like shelves in a catacomb, and the vertical supports become bars imprisoning the elderly who turn into corpses before our eyes, unable to reach the 'offerings' of food placed between the bars. Fritta chose a shaky line here to accentuate the death-throes of the inmates. The style is Expressionist in the extreme, but the method differs from that of Favier's drawing or Taslitzky's *Death of Danielle*. Rather than giving us even an exaggerated *depiction* of the 'boxes',

Fig.17 Bedrich Fritta,
Quarters of the Aged,
*c.*1943, wash

Fritta has *symbolised* their meaning as death-traps for the inmates.

This analysis shows that the artist's personality and goals strongly influenced the manner in which he drew his witness report. But there is an added factor involved, which helps to explain why Fritta's work is so different from that of the other artists we have examined. Most camp artists worked alone, often in secret, and this solitude may have intensified their need to make accurate reports of what they had seen, although they felt free to exaggerate in order to increase the emotional impact and to reveal the truth.[33] On the other hand, at Theresienstadt, a group of artists from among those in the camp – Fritta, Otto Unger, Leo Haas and Felix Bloch – had joined together in an act of organised resistance to the Germans.[34] Leaving pure documentation to artists such as Malvina Schalkova and Charlotte Buresova who did not take part in their secret work, they set out to use an Expressionist style whose conscious goals were not essentially different from those of other camp artists. However, as we shall see, there were a number of characteristics inherent in modern Expressionism which influenced their works in ways they may not have envisaged when they espoused this style. The result is an art which is markedly different from that of other inmates.

The fact that this was a conscious group decision, rather than a coincidental alliance between four Expressionist artists, can be seen in the development of Leo Haas, one of the most highly Expressionist of the artists in the group. In 1939 in Nisko and in some of his early Theresienstadt work, his style is much less exaggerated, and he returned to naturalism in 1945 at Sachsenhausen.[35] The choice of Expressionism was undoubtedly prompted by the revulsion these artists felt against the academic naturalism they continued to use in their 'official' works. Naturalism thus became for them the style of lies rather than a documentary account of the truth. Compounding this revulsion was the feeling that they were in a basically Expressionist situation: they lived in a 'model' camp which masked the true meaning of the camps from the world. It was their duty to strip off this pleasant mask and expose the rotten truth hidden behind it, or as they put it, to encourage each other: 'Tell it like it is.'[36]

This revelatory function of their art can be seen clearly in the works of Fritta and Haas, especially those connected with the visit of the Red Cross to the camp on 23 June 1944 and the making of a film on Theresienstadt in July 1944. In *Film and Reality*,[37] Fritta depicts a sad Jew whose make-up is being applied by a lovely Jewish beautician, a semi-robot organically attached to her table. The film is photographed by another human machine – a movie camera wearing the boots of a Stormtrooper. As sad as the poor Jew looks, the reality hidden by the curtain behind him is still grimmer: death appears there in the form of a skeleton lying in a concentration camp. This work symbolises both the truth behind the lies of the Nazi propaganda film and the story of its production. Written and directed by Jews who had been forced to create it, the film showed concerts, sports, coffee-houses, the non-existent bank and even a garden party – all signs that life in Theresienstadt was ideal and was run by the Jews. After the film was completed, those who had participated in it were shipped to Auschwitz.[38]

Fritta presents a similar approach in *Potemkin-style Shops*. Here the stores built to impress the Red Cross, mockingly labelled '*Parfumerie*' and '*Lebensmittel*', are shown to be false fronts with decomposing corpses behind them.[39] In the foreground, a skeletal couple, embracing before a sloping stone building, are watched from the window by Death – a skeleton behind bars. To understand fully the connection between death and these false fronts, one must realise that to make the camp less crowded before the inspection, the Germans shipped the surplus prisoners, including children, the old and the infirm, to Auschwitz.[40] Fritta's style in these works is exagger-

Fig.18 Leo Haas, *The 'Café'*, *c.*1944, pen and ink and wash

ated and caricatural, far from a documentary treatment of reality, but, as in his *Quarters of the Aged*, he is really 'telling it like it is'.

Haas relates the same story more subtly. In the background of *Ghetto-Swingers* he portrays the 'façade': the band which played to crowds of well-dressed spectators for the Red Cross inspection and the film.[41] Then in the foreground he takes us 'behind-the-scenes', revealing the true story: the hearse used to convey new arrivals and their packages, lines of people arriving or leaving on one of the numerous transports, and an old woman wheeling a corpse cov-

ered with a *tallith*, followed by a woman hiding her face in mourning. The same message is conveyed in *Ghetto Scene*, where the 'stores' are inhabited by the old and dying, while the dead lie on stretchers outside. In the foreground, a blind man walks the street, seeing neither the misery around him nor the naked child dying of malnutrition who extends a bony hand towards him, begging for food.[42] This blind man is a leitmotif in the works of Haas, Fritta and Unger, and undoubtedly represents not only the actual blind people in the ghetto, but the blindness of those who did not realise what was going on.[43]

A few of these blind folk inhabit *The 'Café'* (Fig.18) especially constructed for the Red Cross and the film.[44] Here truth is not juxtaposed to illusion, although the German guard at the window indicates that these people are acting under orders, without choice. Instead, Haas conveys the truth behind the ostensibly joyous scene through his Expressionistic treatment. His café-goers are more skin and bones than flesh, most are old and several are bandaged, showing that force was needed to get them to come. The atmosphere is claustrophobic, the glasses on the tables and on the waitress's tray are empty, and the people are all in a deep depression, staring downwards or blankly in front of them. Few of them converse, most are withdrawn into themselves, and no contact is established even with the waitress, whose low décolletage reveals her dried-up breasts.

Haas's style in these drawings is highly Expressionistic, verging on caricature, in a manner inspired by George Grosz. While this style works in pictures dealing with reality versus illusion, it creates certain problems here, which were equally present in Fritta's depictions of barracks life (Figs 15-16). To understand these problems, one must consider the goals of the German Expressionist artists before and after the First World War – the artists who created the prototypes for such scenes. The Brücke artists, Emil Nolde, Ludwig Meidner, Max Beckmann and Grosz all wanted to satirise the café-goers, to show them up as decadent, dissipated, often ugly people rather than the 'beautiful people' the café-goers considered themselves to be. To this end, their physiognomies were exaggerated and caricatured, and they were often pictured as depressed and withdrawn rather than gay and sociable. The spectator was supposed to be repulsed by this true picture of café-society.[45]

This manner of depiction was used in Theresienstadt, but not necessarily for the same reasons, and this is the crux of the problem. Unger's depiction of the café is closest to the original prototype.[46] There are no Nazi guards and his blue-toned people discuss life while the band plays in the background exactly as if they were in Berlin. Taken out of context, one would say that he and Grosz had the same goals, and that the desiccated man in the foreground was dying of dissipation, not of hunger. Fritta's version is easier to understand. Like Haas, he positions a German guard outside, clarifying his meaning by adding a barbed-wire fence. In the foreground, the Jews, dressed in their Sabbath best, sit like zombies while the band plays under a large clock which ticks the moments of fraud away.[47] There is no communication between the figures: they have been set here as stage props and they behave like objects, giving the lie to the supposedly gay time to be had at a café. Despite the caricatural style, Fritta's message is clear.

Haas's drawing is more problematic, as were Fritta's barracks scenes. Many of the faces could almost be taken for anti-Semitic caricatures, stressing the subhuman qualities of the Jews. In fact, one's first reaction to Haas's café is repulsion rather than sympathy, and if one overlooks the bandages and the Nazi guard in the background, one might misinterpret the scene and feel that Haas was laughing at his fellow inmates. This ambiguity points to a psychological problem which must be taken into account in dealing with these works. Expressionism involves the rendering of one's feelings about a subject into art, but the feelings of a camp inmate are complex. In most camps, Expressionism was held in check and these feelings were channelled in a given direction: the rendition of witness accounts. At Theresienstadt, the pronounced Expressionism of the artists revealed perhaps more than they consciously intended. It revealed their hatred of the situation, and their anger and revulsion not only against the Germans, but also against themselves for yielding to the fraud being perpetuated in the camp – a fraud they helped to promote in order to stay alive. This idea is occasionally expressed in the post-war works of former inmates; in Theresienstadt it existed in the works done in the camp itself. This

Fig.19 Leo Haas, *Hunger*, *c.*1944

explains the Expressionist prototypes chosen by the artists, and the feeling of revulsion that often emerges from their works.

This ambivalence and the problems entailed can be seen through an examination of two works by Haas called *Hunger*. In the first (Fig.19), he concentrated on the revolting sight of people scrounging for food: pushing to get into the hearse that delivered the bread to the camp so as to pick up the last crumbs, scraping the bottom of the barrel and searching the rubbish

Fig.20 Leo Haas, *Hunger, c.*1944, pen and ink and wash, 46 × 61 cm

heaps on all fours for morsels of food.[48] His style is reminiscent of the pictures Grosz and Otto Dix produced on the First World War, and it bears an uncanny resemblance to the paintings Grosz began creating at this time on the destruction of Germany in the Second World War.[49] Haas's picture is a personal comment as well as a document. He has turned the sufferers into subhuman creatures inhabiting a nightmare world that can only repulse the spectator.

On the other hand, his second picture (Fig.20) is a

direct appeal to the spectator.[50] Here the rubbish heap and the soup barrel on the right have been picked clean. Out of the background comes an endless procession of inmates, many of them old, all of them destitute. As they pass through the ruins to wade into the river or cesspool, they hold out their bowls to us begging for food. The style remains the same, the subject is the same, but the goal is different. This work turns outward, rather than inward, translating the plight of the people into a piece of effective propaganda which would make an excellent poster. In the one drawing, Haas himself reacted with repulsion to the ugliness of the situation; in the other, he begs for sympathy and help. Here he not only utilised the two possible faces of Expressionism, but expressed his own ambivalent feelings as well. It is this ambivalence, accentuated by the highly charged Expressionist style, that distinguishes the secret works done at Theresienstadt from the rest of camp art.

The above analysis of the works of camp artists points out several important facts that have not been sufficiently stressed by most researchers. First of all, witnessing is a compound experience: artists are *not* cameras, and their personal reactions to a subject will always 'intrude' on their works, even when they try to be objective. The main vehicle for this intrusion lies in the choice of subject and style. Secondly, since one of the causes of art-work in the camps involves the wish of the artist to preserve or assert his own personality against the impact of Nazi dehumanisation, there was good reason for adding a personal slant to the documentary data. This need was compounded by the fact that straightforward depiction often gave only slight information on what was actually happening in the camps. Third, since many of the artists had been art students or practising artists before the war, they had stored in their memories images from earlier art works which would serve them as prototypes for their camp works. The selection of these models could be fully conscious, or it could be the result of subconscious association and a creative blending of past and present memory-images. Fourth, this artistic past also made available to the artists a choice of styles, and the need to show the truth behind this façade led certain artists to turn more and more to Expressionism, both in camps such as Buchenwald and at Theresienstadt. In doing so, they exposed themselves – as was clear from the case of the Theresienstadt artists – to a fuller expression of their often complex feelings than they may perhaps have desired. The result of their endeavours is that they furnished us not only with documents on how the camps looked but, equally important, on how they felt about being in the camps and undergoing the experience of the Holocaust. Thus, although not always in the way they intended, the artists found a way of involving the spectator on an emotional rather than a purely intellectual level. Finally, in all the examples discussed here – including that of the young Arikha – the artists did not stop being artists just because they had entered the camps. They continued to make stylistic, compositional and iconographical choices even while trying to produce documentary witness reports.

Notes

1. Several attempts to do this have been made, including Z. Amishai-Maisels, *Scenes from the Holocaust* (Israel Museum, Jerusalem, 1981).
2. Zentner points out that although the Germans passionately documented their treatment of the Jews, few photographs of life in the camps have survived [Christian Zentner, *Anmerkungen zu 'Holocaust'* (Munich: Delphin, 1979), p.12]. Costanza suggests that this paucity can be explained by the Nazis' wish that no record be left of the camps [Mary S. Costanza, *The Living Witness* (Free Press, New York, 1982), p.61].
3. This breakdown into categories is based on Janet Blatter, 'Art from the Whirlwind', Janet Blatter and Sybil Milton, *Art of the Holocaust* (Routledge Press, New York, 1981), pp.24-35).
4. Five out of six of the artists on whom pre-internment data are available were trained artists, as is indicated by the biographical material on them. See, for example, *ibid.*, pp.240-68.
5. Boris Taslitzky, *111 Dessins faits à Buchenwald 1944-1945* (Bibliothèque Française, Paris, 1945; republished,

Association française Buchenwald-Dora, Paris, 1978), plates 6, 9-10, 20, 23, 25, 40, 48, 75, 90.

6. *Ibid.*, plates 12, 16, 100, and colour plates 2-5. The same duality of style is found in the works of Zinovii Tolkatchev, who liberated the camps with the Russian Army. His objective recreations of life in the camps are in marked contrast to his more Expressionistic renderings of death [Zinovii Tolkatchev, *Flowers of Oświęcim* (Moses H. Rubin, Cracow, 1947); Zinovii Tolkatchev, *Maydanek* (Spóldzielnia Wydawnicza 'Czytelnik', Warsaw, 1945); Zinovii Tolkatchev (Tolkachyov), *Osventzim* (Mistetztvo, Kiev, 1965), *passim*].

7. Henri Pieck, *Buchenwald* (Het Centrum, Hague, n.d.), pp.6-9, 12-21, 25, 29, 32. All of Pieck's works were done in 1945 as opposed to Taslitzky's which date from 1944 to 1945, and at least some of them (*eg* pp.18-19) were done after the liberation.

8. *Ibid.*, pp.6-7, 24-7, 30.

9. Sean Callahan, ed., *The Photographs of Margaret Bourke-White* (Secker & Warburg, London, 1973), pp.152-3.

10. Blatter and Milton, *Art of the Holocaust*, No.313. For a comparable photograph, see Martin Gilbert, *The Holocaust* (Hill and Wang, New York, 1978), plate 17. The reader should be warned, however, that while similarities to photographs show the objectivity of the artist, too great a similarity often means that he copied – often after the war – from a photograph. Thus Franciszek Wieczorkowski's *Auschwitz 1942*, ostensibly done in 1942 [*Überleben und Widerstehen, Zeichnungen von Häftlingen des Konzentrationslagers Auschwitz 1940-46* (Pahl-Rugenstein, Cologne, 1980), p.11], not only renders all the details with camera-like objectivity, but actually copies a photograph which had been published in one of the earliest books on the camps, *Konzentrationslager* (Graphia, Karlsbad, 1934), opp. p.80, and depicts a scene from Dachau rather than Auschwitz. Wieczorkowski exchanged the original prisoners' garments for striped camp uniforms, gave the inmates numbers and Polish or Jewish badges, added a barbed-wire fence in the background, and 'created' a witness report from Auschwitz. He heightened the difficulty of moving the roller by making the inmates paunchy and stressing the glasses worn by one of them.

11. Pieck, *Buchenwald*, pp.6-7.

12. Blatter and Milton, *Art of the Holocaust*, No. 288. Both these compositions were also used by Adolf Adler, who experienced this form of work in a Nazi labour camp and is apparently haunted by this theme [Erwin Detroy, *Adolf Adler* (in Hebrew) (Rot, Tel Aviv, 1986), pp.19-21, 24, and plates ii-iii, 14, 17].

13. Alexandre Benois, *The Russian School of Painting* (Alfred A. Knopf, New York, 1916), opp. p.132. Ilya Repin (1844-1930) was one of the most famous and most frequently reproduced Russian naturalist painters, and the 'Volga Boatmen' is one of his most popular works. Nansen may also have known Yuri Pimenov's *Give to Heavy Industry* of 1927 (Metropolitan Museum of Art, New York, *Russian and Soviet Painting*, 1977, p.47), which turns Repin's depiction into one of 'voluntary' effort to industrialise Russia. This is suggested by some of the poses and by his use of the background with its sarcastic inscription ostensibly pointing to a better future. A similar ambiguity exists in Pimenov's work, where the industrial complex in the background neither lightens the load of the labourers, nor stops them from literally being burnt by the flames.

14. *Ibid.*, p.82. This fate was actually portrayed by Jerzy Brandhuber in a drawing done in 1946 (*Überleben*, p.65). Brandhuber, who had been an inmate at Auschwitz and Sachsenhausen, built his composition diagonally up the page, so that the effort to pull the weight seems still harder. By portraying only the legs of the workers, he focused attention on his main subject – the fallen prisoner who is being crushed under the roller. Details such as this are typical of post-war works and although Brandhuber may well have witnessed such a scene, he used it here to symbolise the murderous effect of camp labour in a manner meant to clarify what 'mere depiction' had left unsaid. For an even more symbolic post-war version, see Joszef Szajna's *The Roller of Kapo Krankemann (Oświęcim Malarstwo Rzeźba Grafika)* (Wydawnictwo Artystyczno-graficzne, Cracow, 1959), No.42.

15. Blatter and Milton, *Art of the Holocaust*, p.142.

16. *Ibid.*, p.253.

17. See, for instance, Konieczny's comment: 'During the day, I worked with other prisoners on labor details. I drew mostly at night, when the others enjoyed their well-deserved rest' (*ibid.*, p.142).

18. Avigdor Arikha, *Boyhood Drawings Made in Deportation* (Amis de L'Aliya des Jeunes, Paris, 1971), No.5; and interview with the artist. For a similar Expressionist rendering of labour, see Agostino Barbieri's *Arbeit Macht Frei*, which shows a living skeleton pushing a wheelbarrow full of stones [Arturo Benvenuti, *KZ* (Trivigiana, Treviso, 1983), No.10]. Barbieri not only distorts and elongates his figure, but using the dripping ink of his pen, creates the impression that the man, the stones and the background are bleeding. After the war, trying to convey a similar idea, Julian Studnicki simply showed a skeletal corpse leaning against an overturned wheelbarrow, sarcastically entitling the drawing '*Arbeit Macht Frei' (Oświęcim Malarstwo Rzeźba Grafika*, No.11).

19. See the photograph in Gerhard Schoenberner, *The Yellow Star* (Corgi, London, 1969), p.199.

20. Taslitzky, *Buchenwald*, plates 34, 37, and Pieck, *Buchenwald*, pp.10-11. See also Malvina Schalkova's even more orderly depictions of the bunk-beds at Theresienstadt,

where she portrays women exchanging confidences or resting on their crowded but neat beds [Miriam Novitch, *Resistenza Spirituale: Spiritual Resistance 1940-1945* (Commune of Milan, Milan, 1979), pp.83-4; Blatter and Milton, *Art of the Holocaust*, No.69; Miriam Novitch, Lucy Dawidowicz and Tom L. Freudenheim, *Spiritual Resistance: Art from the Concentration Camps, 1940-1945* (Jewish Publication Society of America, Philadelphia, 1981), p.167]. Schalkova's approach was not only posited by the fact that she was documenting Theresienstadt rather than Buchenwald, but by her general tendency to gain control over her ordeal by bringing order and normalcy into camp life at least in pictures.

21. Taslitzky, *Buchenwald*, plates 35-6. See also Benvenuti, *KZ*, No.153 and Odd Nansen, *Day after Day* (Putman, London, 1949), opp. p.184 for other close-ups of the bunks. Taslitzky's 'mound' of sleeping inmates is further emphasised in Reichentál's rendering of the theme [Fr. Reichentál, '*Arbeit Macht Frei*' (Central Union of Jewish Communities of Slovakia, Bratislava, 1946), plate 7].

22. Blatter and Milton, *Art of the Holocaust*, No.112. The only other figure here is the disinterested man at the right; the other inhabitants of the bunks are indicated only by their scattered belongings. As there are only two levels of bunks here, the picture must have been made after the removal of the third level preceding the Red Cross inspection, an act which is documented in a drawing by Helga Weissowa-Hoskova (*ibid.*, No.110).

23. *Ibid.*, No.118; Yad Vashem, *Testimony: Art of the Holocaust* (Winter 1982), p.28.

24. Blatter and Milton, *Art of the Holocaust*, No.216. Blatter states that Favier simply drew what he saw (*ibid.*, p.29), completely disregarding the thematic and stylistic choices the artist made. For a more brutal depiction of the removal of the living dead from the bunks, see Bernard Aldebert, *Chemin de Croix en 50 Stations* (Arthème Fayard, Fontenay-aux-Roses, 1946), p.85, where the corpse-like inmate is yanked out of the bunk under the supervision of a capo, and George Zielezinski's 1943 depiction of the dead falling out of the bunk-beds in *The Hospital* [Fritz Eichenberg, *Dance of Death* (Abbeville, New York, 1983), p.95].

25. Blatter and Milton, *Art of the Holocaust*, No.358.

26. *Arts de France*, No.3 (February 1946), 23.

27. Jacques Gaucheron, 'Entretien avec Boris Taslitzky', *Arts de France*, Nos 29-30 (1950), 58-9, 62-4 (emphasis added). For information on Laurent Casanova, see Françoise Gilot and Carlton Lake, *Life with Picasso* (Signet, New York, 1965), pp.56-7, and for Danielle Casanova, see *Great Soviet Encyclopedia*, 3rd edn (Macmillian, New York, 1976), Vol.11, p.166. She died of typhus.

28. Blatter and Milton, *Art of the Holocaust*, No.99.

29. *Ibid.*, No.97.

30. This detail can be compared with a similar one in the foreground of Taslitzky's *Death of Danielle*. Both artists use the skeletal child as a contrast to the corpse in order to heighten the tragic implications of the scene.

31. Gerald Green, *The Artists of Terezin* (Hawthorn, New York, 1969), p.66. See also his *People at Work* (*ibid.*, p.41), in which he gives an X-ray view into two attics and a cellar which are literally crammed with people. For the official view of the situation, which stresses the efficient use of space, see Peter Kien's 1942 illustration [H. G. Adler, *Die Verheimlichte Wahrheit* (J. C. B. Mohr, Tübingen, 1958), p.147].

32. Green, *Artists of Terezin*, p.109.

33. Exceptions to this rule are Auguste Favier and Pierre Mania, who worked together at Buchenwald, and some of the artists at Gurs and at Les Milles [Blatter and Milton, *Art of the Holocaust*, pp.152, 257; Novitch, *Resistenza Spirituale*, p.21; *Les Camps en Provence: Exil, Internement, Déportation 1933-1944*, special number of *EX* (1984), pp.135, 150-7].

34. Leo Haas, 'The Affair of the Painters in Terezin', *Terezin* (Council of Jewish Communities in the Czech Lands, Prague, 1965), pp.157-61. Karel Fleischmann was not an actual member of the group, but he may have been in contact with it and Haas exhibited his work in the group's exhibitions after the war (*ibid.*, p.161).

35. Green, *Artists of Terezin*, p.6; Blatter and Milton, *Art of the Holocaust*, Nos 46-9, 106-7, 315. Like many other artists, Haas reverted to Expressionism after the war, *ibid.*, No.348; Benvenuti, *KZ*, Nos.87-92, 94; Mirko Tuma, *Ghetto nasich dnu* (Jaroslav Salivar, Prague, 1946), *passim*. Most of these post-war works are not, however, as powerful as the works he did in the camps, as can be seen by comparing similar scenes (e.g. Green, *Artists of Terezin*, p.62 versus Benvenuti, *KZ*, No.90). Fleischmann's works underwent a similar transition from essentially undramatic genre scenes, portraits and landscapes to scenes stressing human emotions and weaknesses [Prague, Zidovske Museum, City of Ceskych Budejovicich, Artists' Association of South Czechoslovakia and Political Prisoners of Prague, *Dra. Karela Fleischmanna*, 2 March-2 April 1947, *passim*; Richard Feder, *Zidovská Tragedie* (Lusk, Kolin, 1947), *passim*]. Fritta, on the other hand, had been a politically conscious artist even before being deported to Theresienstadt [Paul Von Blum, *The Art of Social Conscience* (Universe Books, New York, 1976), p.169].

36. Haas, 'Painters in Terezin', pp.157-61. See also Costanza, *Living Witness*, p.33. For examples of Unger's and Fritta's 'official' works, see Adler, *Die Verheimlichte Wahrheit*, pp.117, 205, 207.

37. Blatter and Milton, *Art of the Holocaust*, No.96.

38. Hans Hofer, 'The Film about Terezin', *Terezin* (see note 34), pp.181-4.

39. Green, *Artists of Terezin*, p.57. This 'false front' aspect was a general characteristic of the camp, as Fleischmann wrote: 'The city is laid out ... according to an exact plan, according to classic urbanistic theories with representative buildings and façades which are reminiscent of Italy. Balance and harmony in space, mass and color, and between them – the human debris that they mixed one hundred times and kneaded into cereal. This city is full of blood, over-crowded and for all that, dead.' (Prague, *Fleischmanna*, quotation after No.91, trans. Susan Landau).

40. Green, *Artists of Terezin*, p.88.

41. *Ibid.*, p.63.

42. *Ibid.*, p.76. The starving child may be one of those from Bialystok described by Green, pp.78-9. This scene should be compared to one of Haas's 'official' works, which depicts a peaceful ghetto scene, with people crowding the street, and women going off to work in the foreground [Emil Utitz, *Psychologie des Lebens im Konzentrationslager Theresienstadt* (A. Sexl, Vienna, 1948), opp. p.32]. See also Haas's later version of this scene, where a bright shining street with gardens hides the overcrowded ghetto (Tuma, *Ghetto*, No.8).

43. Green, *Artists of Terezin*, p.41; Blatter and Milton, *Art of the Holocaust*, No.78; Benvenuti, *KZ*, No.85; Adler, *Die Verheimlichte Wahrheit*, p.262; and the examples discussed below.

44. Green, *Artists of Terezin*, p.77. For the filming of the café scene, see Hofer, 'Film', p.184.

45. For example, Berlin, Nationalgalerie, *Ernst Ludwig Kirchner 1880-1938*, 29 Nov. 1979-20 Jan. 1980, Nos 48, 195; Great Britain, Arts Council, *Painters of the Brücke*, 30 Oct.-6 Dec. 1964, p.16; New York, Solomon R. Guggenheim Museum, *Expressionism: a German Intuition 1905-1920* (1980), pp.55, 279; Thomas Grochowiak, *Ludwig Meidner* (Aurel Bongers, Recklinghausen, 1966), plates 84, 95, 105, 112; London, Marlborough Fine Arts, *Max Bechmann*, Nov. 1974, No.9; Uwe M. Schneede, Georg Bussman and Marina Schneede-Sczesny, *Georg Grosz: His Life and Work* (Universe, New York, 1979), p.87.

46. Blatter and Milton, *Art of the Holocaust*, No.84.

47. Green, *Artists of Terezin*, p.72. This zombie-like quality of the Theresienstadt inmates was described by Fleischmann: 'The human dung heap, the formless mass, lifeless, which finishes playing and doing.' (Prague, *Fleischmanna*, after No.124, trans. Susan Landau).

48. Green, *Artists of Terezin*, p.62. Haas's drawing should be compared to Fleischmann's description of the animal-like behaviour of the starving inmates at meal-time (Prague, *Fleischmanna*, after No.103), and to Fritta's Jews grovelling for food in the dirt (Adler, *Die Verheimlichte Wahrheit*, p.263). See also *Oświęcim Malarstwo Rzeźba Grafika*, No.15, for an Expressionistic post-war rendering of this theme.

49. For example, Hans Hess, *George Grosz* (Yale, New Haven, 1985), pp.57, 82, 210, 219, 225; and Edward Lucie-Smith, *Art of the 1930s: The Age of Anxiety* (Weidenfeld & Nicolson, London, 1985), p.28.

50. Blatter and Milton, *Art of the Holocaust*, No.108.

Professor Ziva Amishai-Maisels is the incumbent of the Alice and Edward G. Winant Chair for Art History, and Head of the Robert and Clarice Smith Center for Art History at the Hebrew University of Jerusalem, Israel. She has written extensively on modern art, concentrating both on modern Jewish art and on Gauguin, and is author of *Depiction and Interpretation: The Influence of the Holocaust on the Visual Arts* (1993).

Ziva Amishai-Maisels

Art Confronts the Holocaust

Art and the Holocaust are concepts that seem to be mutually exclusive; they belong to two entirely different spheres which appear to be separated by an unbridgeable gap. Art has aesthetic rules and strives for beauty and personal expression. It thus seems powerless before the horror and cruelty of the Holocaust in which six million people were slaughtered in ways that can only arouse feelings of disgust and revulsion. Theoreticians have questioned whether it is worthwhile attempting to bridge this chasm: do not the documentary photographs that were taken at the time fulfil the need for visual testimony? Will the artist be able to compete with these black-and-white images which exert such a powerful impact on the spectator? Should the artist attempt to evoke the sense of deep shock that a spectator feels before a pile of skeletal corpses from Buchenwald and Dachau?

Thinkers such as Jean-Paul Sartre and Theodor W. Adorno came to the conclusion that it is neither possible nor warranted for them to do so. Sartre stated that feelings of beauty and horror are mutually exclusive:

A canvas will be beautiful, or it will not be ... Everything is wasted if the spectator flees and fails to return. And if he should come back, punctured eyes and infected wounds – everything – would disintegrate and beauty would never again be reconstituted. Total failure.

Sartre, however, stresses that the danger is even worse if the artist should succeed in turning the 'acts of violence, mutilated corpses and living bodies racked, tortured and burned' into something beautiful, for then he would

betray the anger or grief of man for Beauty ... For a self-willed man in a room with windows overlooking a concentration camp to paint a compote is not serious; his sin is one of negligence. The real crime would be in painting the concentration camp as if it were a compote – in the same spirit of research and experimentation.[1]

Adorno stressed an additional problem:

The so-called artistic representation of naked bodily pain ... of victims felled by rifle butts, contains, however remote,

the potentiality of wringing pleasure from it ... Genocide, when it is made into a cultural possession ... makes it easier to continue playing with the culture that gave it birth ... The distinction between executioner and victim grows hazy.[2]

Despite these admitted dangers, artists were not deterred. Such theories simply did not take into account the creative urge that overrides all limitations, physical, moral or aesthetic. Art, for example, was even created inside the concentration camps despite official prohibition and the absence of materials. Although the artists were aware that such activity endangered their lives, the creative urge was stronger than the fear of death.[3] The main purpose of this art was to provide documentary evidence that would bear witness before the world to the inhuman acts of the Nazis and the inhuman situation in which the inmates lived and died. The artists wished to tear down the impenetrable curtain with which the Nazis cloaked both the camps and the processes of extermination of which, in fact, virtually no photographs have survived. For this reason, no matter how they had been accustomed to painting earlier, now they usually adopted a realistic style that would document conditions as a camera would have done.[4] Karol Konieczny's assertion that he wanted the young 'to know how it was, so that they understand, and will not allow such conditions to ever be repeated in the future',[5] is one that would be stated by many artists, both inside and outside the camps, and constitutes one of the main goals of non-inmate art that deals with the Holocaust. By stirring the conscience of the world and keeping the memory of the Holocaust alive, artists wished to make sure that such a monstrous event would never happen again.

Aside from the inmates, other groups of artists scarred by the Holocaust also created art to document their experiences. Refugees who fled the Nazis in the 1930s and during the war tried through their art to open the eyes of the inhabitants of the host countries to the dreadful conditions current in Germany and Occupied Europe and to incite them to action to save those still caught in the Nazi web. Their sense of impotence to rescue others, and the lack of understanding they encountered in the spectators, frustrated and embittered them, reinforced their feelings of guilt that by succeeding to escape, they had abandoned their brothers. However, unlike the inmates, they felt free to use their own styles and their own iconographies to express their message, often preferring a strong expressionism to a matter-of-fact realism in order to shock the spectators out of their complacence.[6]

The guilt feelings of the camp survivors were similar in many ways to those of the refugees. But although they too tried to document what they had experienced, their motivation was different from that of either the camp artists or the refugees. After their release, they re-created their experiences in order to achieve catharsis: many of them obsessively reworked the same themes again and again, treating them with increasing expressionism as they progressed. Shortly after their liberation, they simply described the difficult conditions of life in the camps and ghettos. Gradually, however, they also began to express the rage and deep pain they had been repressing, which they could safely release only after their liberation: had they expressed these feelings in their camp works, the psychological spill-over of their anger or despair into their lives could have been self-destructive. Their post-war art thus became a means of freeing and purifying themselves from feelings and sights that haunted their dreams and were too difficult to bear.[7] Subsequently, some of these artists felt that they had succeeded in freeing themselves from their bitter experiences and turned to more carefree subjects and to abstract art; but many sooner or later returned to dealing with the Holocaust because they were unable to escape the profound influence of their trauma. Some of them, such as Samuel Bak, admitted that the memory of the Holocaust had even permeated their abstract works, and that it was preferable to admit the influence than to fight it.[8]

Other artist-witnesses – partisans or camp liberators – also felt a strong urge to document the horrors they had seen and to arouse public anger against the perpetrators of the Holocaust. This desire was sometimes so powerful that the camp liberators felt impelled, at the very time that the scenes were being photographed and documented in newsreels, to draw the mounds of bodies and the skeletally thin, scarcely living survivors.[9]

During 1944 - 5 artists who had no contact with the camps also became indirect witnesses of the Holocaust through the agency of newspapers, magazines and cinema newsreels which disseminated images of the horrors discovered when the camps were liberated. The Holocaust had penetrated so deeply into the communications media that even a fashion journal such as *Vogue* contained an article with Lee Miller's photographs documenting the atrocities of Buchenwald.[10] The impact of these photographs and films was so strong that many artists felt the need to react to them in their art. Instead of copying the photographs in a realistic manner, some of the artists adapted them to their own iconography and style, creating reactions to, and interpretations of, the Holocaust that were very different from those generated by the actual witnesses.

Such photographs and, indeed, the very concept of the Holocaust had repercussions far beyond the time-span of their original impact. Artists not personally involved in the Holocaust continued to respond to these images during the 1950s, although they often camouflaged their reactions so that their meaning would not be obvious.[11] In the 1960s, a new surge of more open responses to the problems and images of the Holocaust was triggered by the Eichmann trial; and, as this exhibition shows, they continue to be created to this day. Moreover, during the present period, a second and third generation of artists have begun to react to the Holocaust, some of whom are children or grandchildren of survivors.

The recognition that the Holocaust is an event that

Fig.21 Zoran Music, *Dachau*, 1945, bistre, 21 × 30 cm

cannot be ignored is common to artists of all these groups and generations. For many of them, the Holocaust has transcended its original meaning and has become a symbol of the tragedy of the modern world. Through their treatment of the subject, they warn of the dangers that reside in hatred, mass murder and the unbridled and immoral use of technology. It must be emphasised that the different ways in which these artists reacted to the Holocaust was also affected by their personalities, their nationalities, their social and religious affiliations, and their approaches to art, including their individual style and iconography.

In addressing the subject of the Holocaust, non-inmate artists encountered different problems from those that confronted the camp artists. Although the latter group planned their drawings, at least unconsciously, according to the aesthetic concepts they had learned before entering the camps, they saw their creations primarily as documents rather than as art. On the other hand, non-inmate artists envisaged their works primarily as art rather than as documents, and dedicated a great deal of conscious thought to aesthetic considerations. In order to communicate their messages, they had to ensure that the spectators would look at their works and not turn away in rejection, as Sartre had warned they might do. These artists had to devise tactics that would capture the attention of the spectator, force him or her to examine the work of art and thus confront the subject of the Holocaust.

Whereas some artists chose primarily stylistic means to draw the spectator into their works, others communicated their messages by other methods: they used known artistic models, such as Goya's *Third of May 1808*, or commonly accepted images or symbols.[12] In the course of time, these strategies came to be modified according to the different types of reaction the artists wished to elicit from the spectator. A discussion of the manner in which the depiction of a few familiar Holocaust subjects developed helps to clarify the ways in which artists solved the problems of communication with the spectator without completely breaking the aesthetic rules.

One of the most striking, but aesthetically difficult, visual images to emerge from the Holocaust was that of the skeletally thin corpses discovered scattered or in piles when the camps were liberated. These corpses were portrayed by inmates, liberators and survivors, as well as by artists who had seen them only in photographs and newsreels. This image became one of the central themes – even almost a symbol – of the Holocaust.[13]

Witnesses tended to depict the dead in a straight-forward manner as individuals rather than as mounds of corpses. For instance, during his last months of imprisonment in Dachau in 1945, Zoran Music did a series of drawings of dead bodies. Immediately after his liberation, he repeated several of them, making them more and more expressive. These drawings are thus both witness reports and attempts by the artist to achieve catharsis from the traumatic sights that hypnotised him. Music usually depicted four to six nude skeletal corpses, lying on the ground or in open coffins, with brutal realism (Fig.21): their genitals are exposed and their bodies tossed one on the other so that the feet of one collide with the head of the other. Most shocking of all – they sometimes seem to be still alive: they establish eye contact with the spectator, raise an arm in self-defence, or turn towards each other in conversation or aggression. Music explained:

In the last couple of months at Dachau, people were dying in droves ... Every morning you noticed that this one and that one had died ... I became fascinated by these heaps of bodies ... because they had a kind of ... tragic beauty. Some of them weren't quite dead, their limbs still moved and their eyes followed you round, begging for help. Then, during the night, a little snow would fall. The heap wouldn't move again.[14]

Both the description and the depictions are purposely difficult to absorb, and were it not for the expressiveness of some of Music's drawings, their delicate lines and lack of colour and three-dimensionality, most spectators would follow Sartre's dictum and avert their eyes.

In the same year, Pablo Picasso, inspired by photographs and possibly by a 1944 film on the liberation of Maidanek, attempted an entirely different solution to the problem of depicting the corpses in *The Charnel House* (Fig.22).[15] Instead of showing anonymous Holocaust victims as they appeared in the photographs, Picasso chose to concentrate specifically on the destruction of the family unit. The father appears face down with his head on the right and his legs on the left; his protruding ribs are stressed; and his hands are tied behind his back and pulled up behind him almost in the centre of the picture. The mother lies on him, her head to the left with her hand raised to her chin; her breasts and stomach are bloated; and her legs are on the right. The baby lies on the father, and is situated under the mother's head; he raises his palms to catch or protect himself from the blood that

spills from her breast instead of milk. The connection to the Holocaust is suggested through the father's figure: his arms are tied in the manner found in photographs of torture and execution;[16] his body and face are emaciated; and at the right there is a hint of flames.

To suggest a mass of bodies rather than just a single family, Picasso fragmented the figures by means of white, grey and black planes in a way that makes it hard for us to decipher how many bodies are actually portrayed. We identify a head here, hands there, with no connection between them, as if we were looking at a mound of corpses of the type discovered in the camps.[17] However, the stylised semi-abstraction soft-

ens the horror with which we react to photographs or to Music's documentary drawings. Rather than turning from the painting with revulsion, we are drawn into the picture by our need to reorganise in our minds the parts of the bodies we have succeeded in identifying and thus to make sense out of what we perceive. In this way, Picasso catches us on an intellectual level, and the emotional reaction occurs only after we have solved the visual puzzle.

To complicate the decipherment of the painting's meaning, Picasso does not add common identifying signs of the concentration camp, such as the barbed-wire fence. On the contrary, he places the bodies in a narrow room, under a table which holds simple house-

Fig.22 Pablo Picasso, *The Charnel House*, 1945, oil and charcoal on canvas, 1.99×2.50 m

hold utensils of the sort he had painted in Paris during and immediately after the Occupation, thus creating in his own mind a connection between the Holocaust and his own experiences under the Nazis. However, since he uses the table as part of his strategy to involve us intellectually in the picture, Picasso leaves us free to understand its connection to the corpses as we wish. We ask ourselves why these figures are lying under the table: were they killed in a house which is going up in flames? Or does the distinction between the clean drawing of the table and the utensils and the fragmented treatment of the painted figures mean that they belong to different worlds? And what do the two worlds connote in this context? Everyone can arrive at a different explanation. The important thing is that the spectator, who may be revolted by the photographs and by Music's drawings to the point of refusing to look at them or even to think about them, will delve into the painting in an attempt to solve its puzzles, and will thus begin to cope with the Holocaust and the problems it raises.

Yet this type of treatment also raises questions: is there not a danger here that the artist is doing just what Sartre warned against, betraying the anger or grief of man for beauty? Does not the aesthetic distance Picasso created with such skill by means of semi-abstraction and the use of only black, white and grey, *overly* protect the spectator from the full impact of the Holocaust? Can the lessons of the Holocaust be taught in such a distanced manner, or does one need to make the confrontation more brutal to drive the facts home to the spectator?

The answers to these questions depend to a great extent on the period when the picture was painted. Christian Zervos wrote that Picasso created *The Charnel House*

to show the terror of man at the sight of the many corpses that weigh on his heart, and his horror of disgust in the face of a world of murderers, of fire and filth, a world of ruins which ceaselessly reflects his [man's] own image covered with blood.[18]

At the time the work was created, many people – Picasso included – had already been amply shocked by the events they had witnessed either first-hand or through photographs and newsreels. What was needed was some way of transcending the emotional trauma, of confronting the Holocaust more coolly in order to grasp the meaning of what had happened and to learn from it. Picasso's response, as Zervos relates, had been purely emotional, but in order to turn these emotions into an expressive work of art, he needed to establish a distance from the images. This was also the only means by which he could address a war-weary, overly emotionally charged public, already tiring of realistic depictions of the horrors of the war.

This last point is worth stressing: given that it is impossible to react indefinitely, even to a catastrophe, at full emotional pitch, there were additional reasons why the public began to recoil from artistic representations of the Holocaust shortly after the war. Not only did the Holocaust pose too many embarrassing questions that made people profoundly uncomfortable, but it was widely felt that the realistic or expressionistic depiction of Holocaust victims was akin to harping on old wounds. It was time, surely, to bury such memories, get on with life, and reconstruct a better world.[19] Picasso, in a sense, anticipated this reaction: the subtlety and unemotional tone of his painting were specifically constructed to suck the spectator into the subject without his being aware of it, and thus to reach beyond his barriers and his immediate impulse to turn away. Yet later generations for whom the Holocaust was not a live and traumatic memory could – and did – miss the point of this painting. Its neutral title and aesthetic distance enabled certain art historians to dissociate *The Charnel House* from the Holocaust, and to explain that it dealt instead with war in general, or with the Spanish Civil War in particular, concepts they could more easily assimilate.[20]

The fact that artists in the 1950s as a rule preferred not to label their works with Holocaust titles or to

admit that they were even dealing with this subject, does not mean, however, that they ceased to be influenced by it. For instance, Leonard Baskin's series of *Dead Man* can be said to have begun with a 1949 woodcut of a skeletally thin corpse, inspired in part by the many Holocaust photographs he had collected, but entitled *Dead Worker*.[21] Unable to use these photographs in a direct manner, Baskin sought different types of images through which he could confront his Holocaust-induced trauma, without even having to acknowledge to himself that he was doing so. He found these images in late Gothic sculpture and in the corpses of Pompeii, learning to cover the skeletal frames with soft rounded flesh and to give their faces a smiling serenity in the face of death. Only in his bronze *Dead Man* (Fig.23) does he suggest the agony of dying: these figures appear ravaged by time, their skin rough and seemingly charred, and their arms and feet are missing. Without being aware of the context in which they were done, of Baskin's interests and personal history, the association of these works with the Holocaust can be ignored, and they can be regarded simply as generalised images of death – a notion the artist himself prefers.

In the following decades, it became clear to many artists that works such as Picasso's *The Charnel House* were not fulfilling their purpose either of forcing a confrontation with the Holocaust or of teaching its lessons, and that statues such as Baskin's *Dead Men*, although still responding to the Holocaust on a personal, perhaps unconscious, level, were not even attempting to pursue such aims. More importantly, by the end of the 1960s, it was obvious that the world had learnt nothing from the Holocaust: wars, massacres and even genocide proceeded apace. Some artists began to envisage a more striking use of Holocaust imagery which would be calculated to shock rather than entice the spectator into contemplation.

Zoran Music, for example, after recovering from his Dachau experience, had turned to depictions of child-

Fig.23 Leonard Baskin, *Dead Man*, 1952, bronze, length 46 cm

like peasant scenes and landscapes, and later to abstraction. Gradually, however, his works became more sombre, and even his abstract compositions contained suggestions of skulls. In the 1970s he based his series *We Are Not the Last* on his Dachau drawings, explaining both his return to them and his title:

The experiences of these last troubled years which demanded a state of anguish, forced me down this path. How often did we say in Dachau that such things should never be repeated in this world! They are being repeated. This means that the horrible is in Man himself and not only in a specific society.[22]

Since his present goal was no longer to document atrocity, but – from the depths of despair – to warn mankind of the future and persuade it to change its ways, Music's paintings of the 1970s do not merely repeat his Dachau drawings, but develop them in new, strongly expressive and colouristic ways.

In many of these paintings, he brings us into immediate contact with the corpses through close-ups that focus on their heads and torsos, which are usually cut off directly below the exposed genitals (Col.Fig.34). These corpses, already slightly decomposed, are painted in beige with the details often picked out in a sienna reminiscent of dried blood. To reinforce the message that the Holocaust victims were not the last to die in war and genocide, Music sets the corpses against deep blue or red backgrounds, elevating them into symbols beyond the original event while still clearly evoking it. Rather than lying on the ground, as in the drawings, his corpses rise up before us, trying to communicate both with one another and with the spectator. Sometimes they kneel in prayer, calling on God to save themselves and mankind. Elsewhere the artist builds up masses of corpses, piled endlessly one on the other, so that the ground seems literally covered with them. This endless sea of figures is no longer merely an image of the Holocaust, but of Everyman as victim and of the future that awaits mankind if it does not mend its ways.

As it became increasingly evident during the next decade that the lessons of the Holocaust had still not been learned, with denials in certain quarters that it had ever occurred, Robert Morris, in a series of untitled works which he painted between 1985 and 1987, decided to put *all* the horror back into the subject. It is important to note that the first of these works were purposely and provocatively made for the *Documenta 8* exhibition in Germany, the defined theme of which was the 'historical and social dimension of art', with the focus on its social responsibilities.[23] Morris wrote that he wished to 'counter the pernicious amnesia that already is at work softening the contours of this mark on our time'.[24] In several of his Holocaust works, therefore, he returned to the documentary photographs of corpses found in the camps – images that he himself, as a youth, could not bear to look at – and enlarged them to almost life-size figures (Col.Fig.28). He set them in frames, some of them arched to recall the shape of the crematorium ovens. To stress the sadistic brutality of the act of mass murder, Morris decorated these frames with cat-o'-nine-tail whips, machine parts, fists, penises and weapons. To heighten the already strong level of horror, he coloured the bodies with strong reds, oranges, yellows and browns to evoke flames, covered them with encaustic applied by heating the wax with a blowtorch, and burned the borders and even parts of the photographic images themselves. In this way he managed both to depict and re-enact the burning of the bodies, and to create some of the harshest images of Hell ever portrayed. In the face of a work such as this it is impossible to preserve the mood of comfortable distancing generated by Picasso. Morris arouses in the spectator an emotional experience similar to that provoked by the original contact with the corpses: he kicks us sharply in the gut with an unbearable force.

Yet at the same time Morris emphasises the aesthetic factor. His work involves an interplay of materials, colours and shapes that hypnotises the spectator even while the subject matter repels him or her. Here again questions are raised: will the spectator flee and refuse to return, as Sartre suggested? Will he return repeatedly and discover each time new facts that contribute to his understanding of the Holocaust, as the artist intended? Or will he return only to derive pleasure from the sadism involved, as Adorno warned? And was the action of the artist himself in burning the photographic images not inherently sadistic? These questions are by no means easy to answer. On the one hand, the reaction of every spectator to these works is different, doubtless covering the entire gamut of sensations suggested above. On the other hand, we must judge the artist here not only by these specific works but by their context: Morris created them following a series dealing with nuclear war, and he regarded both series as warnings against a future apocalypse. Moreover, he continued to produce less violent works involving the Holocaust after finishing this series (see below).[25]

A comparison of the above works reveals the differences that result from the varying goals of the artists, their personalities and the dates of the work. Music worked at first as a witness during the Holocaust, attempting to record data. Picasso tried to engage the spectator on an intellectual level, taking for granted both his knowledge of the Holocaust and his need to go beyond the emotional level to understand its diverse aspects. In the 1950s, artists such as Baskin generalised the images and hid their meanings, so that an emotional gap was created between the original impetus for the work and its final expression. In the 1970s and 1980s, artists such as Music and Morris felt that this aesthetic distancing had undermined the ability of the works to function meaningfully: almost half a century later, the public had either forgotten the Holocaust or had become accustomed and therefore indifferent to its atrocities. In the belief that such an attitude could cause another Holocaust, they returned to a more expressionistic treatment of the subject, restoring emotional content to the depiction to shock the spectator into awareness.

The problems discussed so far have been primarily aesthetic, having to do with the use of style to elicit the spectator's emotional engagement or his intellectually distanced reaction. However, the artists' need to communicate with the spectator also brought about an entirely different development, based on iconography. In order to communicate one must speak an understandable language: in art, to be visually effective and not rely only on explanatory titles, one must use familiar images with accepted meanings. There were several directions in which this Holocaust iconography developed.

The easiest way to create clearcut Holocaust images was to extract them from the camp experience. Thus instead of depicting all the details of camp life and death, as an inmate would do in attempting to produce *documents*, artists who had not been in the camps preferred to use a *standard depiction* that would be readily recognisable.[26] The representations needed to fulfil certain criteria to be easily read and have a potent effect. First, they had to encapsulate the experience into a single image which would resound meaningfully for the spectator because it was based either visually or conceptually on what he or she knew about the Holocaust. Second, these images had to be used in such a way as to arouse strong emotions but not excessive repulsion.

The image of the concentration camp became encapsulated, for example, in a depiction of an inmate behind barbed wire, with or without other relevant details, such as striped uniforms, shaven heads, barracks, watchtowers, etc. This extremely readable symbolism developed in the mid-1930s and is still current today, preserving its meaning even in the most minimalistic treatments. One of the earliest visual renderings of the idea was Peter Nikl's drawing for *Simpl* of 14 November 1934, which depicts the head of a man behind barbed wire, with inmates labouring under guard behind him.[27] This drawing was done at the time of the earliest publications on the camps that the Germans had begun to construct in 1933.[28] However, rather than choosing images that derived from such early documents, or from the testimony of political prisoners who had been freed from the camps in the 1930s,[29] Nikl and other artists throughout the world opted for an image that would be readily understandable to those with *minimal* knowledge of the subject. Before people were aware of what was happening *in* the camps, it was conceptually clear that the latter were surrounded by a fence of barbed wire; and artists realised that the use of such wire to separate the inmates from the spectator would command instant recognition. This is also the reason why this image has remained so prevalent: more specific knowledge is needed to recognise, for instance, the gates of Auschwitz or the bunk-beds,[30] but the image of the inmate behind barbed wire strikes an immediate chord in the spectator, and is not readily replaceable as a clearcut symbol of the concentration camp itself.

The mindset of the artist in creating this image can be seen in a drawing by George Grosz from 1941 (Col.Fig.29). Grosz had been told in detail what was occurring in the camps by Hans Borchardt, who had been interned in Dachau and had come to the United States in 1937, four years before Grosz made his drawing. Whereas Grosz reported Borchardt's testimony on the sufferings of daily life in the camp in writing, he does not describe them in his drawings; instead he portrays only the simple state of a bored and lonely human being in the camp.[31] Within the barbed-wire fence an inmate walks round and round until his footsteps form a circle in the mud. His hands are held, or perhaps tied, behind his back; he has a number on his uniform, his hair is short and signs of malnutrition and pain appear on his face. The barbed-wire fence that surrounds him is the only clear sign that he is in a camp.[32]

The image of an inmate standing behind a barbed-wire fence was so common at the end of the war that it even influenced the photographers who visited the camps after the liberation: most of them preferred to photograph the inmates behind barbed wire, thus moving the image from art into reality, and reinforc-

ing it as a documentary image in the public mind. This was so accepted that from 1945 on, even a single strand of barbed wire in front of a figure, a head or a hand, was enough to represent the camp, and was indeed used in this manner in posters and books.[33] Its continuing potency can be seen in the drawing Fernand Léger made in 1955 to mark the tenth anniversary of the liberation of the camps (Fig.24). The hand of a Holocaust survivor is raised here towards a shining sun – a symbol of salvation. His identity is suggested by his striped sleeve, but would not be obvious without the strands of barbed wire that appear in front of and behind his hand. On the wrist of the second hand in the foreground, there is a line that can be understood either as barbed wire or as the edge of a sleeve. Depending on how this line is interpreted, the hand can be seen either as belonging to a second prisoner or to a camp liberator. In this minimalist rendering, Léger suggests to the spectator a clear image of the Holocaust and the liberation.

So accepted was this image that barbed wire, even without a prisoner, was used to symbolise the Holocaust. For instance, Seymour Lipton composed his statue of *The Martyr* of 1948 from strands of metal, the spiked shapes of which recall barbed wire, creating a powerful image of Holocaust suffering which also has overtones of Christ's crown of thorns.[34] In the early 1960s, Igael Tumarkin used barbed wire in his abstract works to evoke the Holocaust, and from the end of the 1970s, this symbol seemed so unmistakable to him that he began to use it in other political contexts in order to lend a Holocaust connotation to contemporary events.[35]

Other widespread symbols of the Holocaust also demanded very little knowledge from the spectators: cattle-cars and railway lines were employed to symbolise the deportations; gaunt, skeletally thin but living figures were identified immediately as survivors; and children, sometimes accompanied by their mothers, were used to express the innocence of the Holocaust's victims.[36] However, the two Holocaust symbols that became as omnipresent and as immediately identifiable as barbed wire were the heaps of skeletally thin corpses that were all too familiar from the documentary photographs, and the chimney, which symbolised the most idiosyncratic form of Holocaust murder – death in the gas chamber and the burning of the corpses in the crematorium. The artistic representation of these themes raises intense aesthetic problems.

The subject of gassing and cremation was only rarely depicted by inmates during their stay in the camps. Most of them neither saw nor knew exactly what was happening, and those who did see the gas chambers in operation were usually soon sent to die there in their turn. Moreover, there were no prior artistic prototypes to help artists outside the camps to cope with this unimaginable subject, as there were for other forms of Holocaust death, such as shooting and hanging.[37] Since artists found it extremely hard to find an effective method of handling a theme that would not immediately repel the spectator, they seldom portrayed it.[38]

An example of a relatively low-key depiction of this subject will reveal some of the problems. Lea Grundig's *Treblianca* of 1943-4 was included in her series *In the Valley of Slaughter*, in which she tried to awaken the inhabitants of Palestine and the British mandate authority to the situation in the camps of Europe (Fig.25).[39] Grundig, a refugee from Germany, learned of what was occurring in the camps through communist sources who were extremely well informed. She depicted a cell crowded to overflowing with naked women, children and old people. In their terror they hold on to each other, their faces expressing their fear, or fall dying to the ground. On the one hand, they arouse our sympathy: Grundig specifically chose women, one of whom is pregnant, children and the aged in order to stress their innocence and helplessness. On the other hand, their condition arouses revulsion and anger: revulsion because of their unaesthetic situation, and anger against those who have brought them to this state. Grundig indeed intended to rouse

the spectators in this way in order to achieve her goal: by forcing them to confront the ugly facts of the Holocaust, she hoped to inspire them to save the Jews from this horrible fate.[40]

Most spectators find it painful to look at Grundig's depiction of the gas chamber for any length of time. It is thus not surprising that this kind of representation became uncommon by the 1950s, and that artists

Fig.24 Fernand Léger, *Untitled*, 1955. From *La Déportation* (Le Patriote Résistant, Fédération Nationale des Déportés et Internés Résistants et Patriotes, Paris, 1967)

Fig.25 Lea Grundig,
Treblianca, *c*.1943 - 4,
drawing in pencil, ink
and wash

sought other ways to deal with the subject. The most accepted method was to use the 'non-threatening' symbol associated with this mode of death to convey the idea of both gassing and burning: the crematorium chimney. These ominous chimneys, often belching flames or yellow smoke, can be found in many camp drawings; and they struck the liberators with such force that they immediately adopted them as a symbol of the camps. Several of the camps themselves preserved the chimneys as part of their memorialisation of the Holocaust, and it soon became a standard element in other Holocaust memorials.[41] In fact, so acceptable was it and so deeply did it penetrate – especially into the Jewish consciousness – that any smokestack, whether in life or in art, could immediately call forth Holocaust associations.[42]

The chimney became a particularly important Holocaust symbol in the art of survivors, whether or not they had experienced the spectacle at first-hand. Thus, for instance, Naftali Bezem, Samuel Bak and Friedensreich Hundertwasser, who had never actually seen the chimneys in operation, found it relatively easy to integrate this explicit Holocaust symbol into their own personal iconographies. Hundertwasser's *Blood Garden: Houses with Yellow Smoke* of 1962 - 3 (Col.Fig.31) presents a completely symbolic depiction of the camps: multi-storeyed barracks are set in the midst of one of his favourite Holocaust motifs, the fenced-in blood garden, suggesting that there is no escape from the deadly camps. To stress the type of killing practised here, he adds chimneys belching insidious yellow smoke: one is set on the roof of the barracks and the other at the corner of the camp gate, in the foreground. The yellow smoke has a chilling effect: as it passes through the red blood-filled windows of the house in the foreground, it turns them black, as though the life within them had been burnt in the crematorium. In this way Hundertwasser presents an image of Holocaust death which neither repels nor angers the spectator, and which keeps him looking at the work of art trying to decipher its meaning.[43]

In the mid-1980s artists began to feel that the kind of aesthetic distance engendered by such images was so great that the works were no longer capable of arousing emotional reactions, specifically because all suggestion of atrocity had disappeared. These artists decided to put the figure back into the work, and with it the horror. We have already seen how Robert Morris combined Holocaust corpses with the arched shape of the crematorium ovens and the notion of burning, to produce excruciating but riveting images. R. B. Kitaj elected to continue to use the chimney's protective distance, but to merge it both with the victim and with other associations. In *Passion 1940 - 1945: Girl/Plume* of 1985 (see front cover), he constructed a chimney that also recalls the shape of a coffin. Into it, as in a box, he placed a fragile, pale girl who automatically arouses the spectators' pity, especially as they follow the winding yellow flame-like line of smoke that coils over her body and obliterates her face as a suggestion that she is being gassed or cremated. This image recalls Paul Celan's poem, *Death Fugue*, written in 1945 in a labour camp, in which the murdered and cremated Shulamith is wafted to the sky as smoke, or as Celan puts it: 'as smoke you will rise into air / then a grave you will have in the clouds there one lies unconfined'.[44] In this image, Kitaj strikes the balance between confrontation and artistic norms, allowing the spectators to continue looking at the work, but engaging them emotionally rather than only intellectually.

We have reviewed some of the methods chosen by artists to cope with the problem of portraying the Holocaust, either directly or by means of symbols. Many artists, however, felt a need not only to document or to describe the events but also to understand them and to learn from them moral lessons for the present and the future. This was suggested in the analysis of some of the above-mentioned works, especially those of Morris and Music, but the point must now be investigated in greater depth.

The need to make events comprehensible began

even before the Nazis rose to power, when artists recognised the potential dangers of their political platform, and tried to warn the public against its likely consequences. For example, to make the public understand the true nature of the Nazis, John Heartfield portrayed them as animals, monsters and symbols of death. After Hitler assumed office in 1933, several artists began to worry about the fate of Jews under the Nazis: Marc Chagall depicted a Jew thrown out of Eastern and Western Europe in his *Solitude* (1933), while Jacques Lipchitz prayed through his sculpture *David and Goliath* that the Jewish David would conquer the Nazi Goliath, the latter being identified by the swastika engraved on his chest.[45] These works did not attempt to depict a given situation but to warn the public, to make it understand the meaning of what was happening, and to incite it to action. This goal of communication necessitated the use of a symbolic language of images that were familiar to everyone.

Such was the thinking that motivated the creation of one of the earliest and most popular interpretative Holocaust symbols, the use of the Passion and Crucifixion of Christ to symbolise the sufferings of the Jews and their murder by the Nazis. This imagery was employed in the 1930s by Chagall and by German Christian anti-Fascist artists such as Otto Pankok. In their works, the Jewishness of Jesus is suggested in several ways: Pankok portrays him with Semitic facial features which are markedly different from those of the Aryans who torture him; in other works the INRI sign on the cross whereby Jesus of Nazareth is proclaimed king of the Jews is written out in full in German or in Hebrew letters; and Chagall visually identifies Christ with modern Jews by clothing him in a prayer-shawl or phylacteries, and by surrounding him with scenes of pogroms and Nazi desecration (see Col.Fig.27).[46] This emphasis on the Jewishness of Jesus aroused sharp reactions among the Nazis who preferred to think of him as being of pure Aryan descent. The goal of these German artists, however, was not

simply to upset the Nazis, but to warn Christians that in killing Jews – either actively or by not opposing their murder – they were crucifying Christ anew, as he was a member of the same race and people as present-day Jews. By using a symbol taken from the Christian symbolic vocabulary, the artists hoped to arouse the Christian public against the Nazis' deeds.

When it became obvious that this goal would not be achieved, a subtle change occurred in the use of Christological imagery. Artists now used the Crucifixion as a means of blaming Christians for the Holocaust. Thus, for example, Joseph Foshko depicted the crucifixion of an old Jew wrapped in a prayer-shawl and wrote under him words that invert those of Jesus on the cross: 'Forgive them NOT, Father, for they KNOW what they do.'[47] This blame was also directed by several artists, both Jews and Christians, against the Church which stood by or actively aided the Nazis in their war against the Jews.[48] Thus the symbol which was intended to warn a Christian audience to prevent the catastrophe was later used to blame both the Church and Christians for the Holocaust.

Other biblical images conveyed different ways of understanding the meaning of the Holocaust. Two of these – the suffering of Job and the Sacrifice of Isaac – proved particularly popular as they were deemed appropriate archetypes for the victims.[49] The more immediately relevant was that of Job, the blameless righteous man who, suddenly and senselessly, was deprived of his possessions, his children and his health, and thus seemed a veritable prototype of the innocent Holocaust victims who had no control over the evils that befell them. The aptness of this symbol was appreciated both by artists who were trapped by the Nazis and by those who were safely beyond their reach. One of the most striking of these images is Ivan Mestrović's statue of 1945 in which Job is as emaciated as an inmate, and from the depths of his physical and psychic torments calls on God to explain why he has been punished (Fig.26). The biblical dialogue between Job and God following this demand was

Fig.26 Ivan Mestrović,
Job, 1945, bronze,
1.24 × 1.02 × 1.02 m

another fundamental reason for using this image, as it
enabled the artist to explore the various reactions that
Job – and, by extension, the Holocaust victim – might
have to his sufferings. Artists such as Mestrović
showed Job blaming God and calling Him to judg-
ment. Others showed Job listening in silence to God's
answer to this charge, or underlined either his loss of
belief and subsequent despair or his unshaken continuing faith which would lead to his health, family and
wealth being restored to him.[50]

These treatments of Job are traditional and evolve
from the biblical text itself. On the other hand, the
use that artists made of the Sacrifice of Isaac is completely anti-traditional. Since the victims of the
Holocaust were not rescued by a miracle, as happened
to Isaac, there was a need to fit the signifying symbol
to the signified events. One of the most successful
solutions to this problem is found in Mordecai Ardon's
Sarah of 1947, in which Isaac's pale, bloodless body
lies *dead* on the altar (Col.Fig.30). Beside him, Sarah
raises her head to cry out against God, while a tiny
Abraham sits mourning helplessly at the bottom left,
the ladder which signifies his connection with God
lying uselessly on the ground, as God had not saved
Isaac. In such works, artists utilised the Sacrifice of
Isaac not in the traditional way to express unques-
tioning faith in God, but rather to vent their anger
against a God who had failed to save His people and
allowed the Holocaust to happen.[51]

This use of the images of Job and the Sacrifice of
Isaac alternately to affirm faith in God and to blame
Him for the Holocaust are in many ways opposite
sides of the same coin. They reflect in fact, the contra-
dictory reactions of the biblical Job, who at first
blames God and finally submits and reaffirms his
faith. Both posit a personal relationship between man
and God and the possibility of a dialogue between
them. Thus both approaches have traditional roots in
Judaism, and also parallels in Jewish theological writings and literature about the Holocaust.

A related way of expressing continued faith in

adversity was through a return to Jewish traditions
and an open avowal of Jewish identity. The more the
Nazis hounded the Jews, the more artists who had
abandoned their religion in their youth returned to
their Jewish roots. Thus, in the 1920s, Ludwig
Meidner, in Germany, stressed his Jewish character
both in writing and by portraying Jews at worship
wrapped in prayer-shawls. During the 1930s he
became gradually more and more orthodox, signing
his works in Hebrew and with the Jewish date. He
continued to do so after he found refuge in England,
and stopped only after he returned to Germany in
1952.[52]

One of the strongest expressions of Jewish faith in
adversity to be created in a Holocaust context is
Lipchitz's *Prayer* of 1943 (Fig.35). Although the entire
centre of the body of the old bearded Jew has been
blown open and his legs are eaten away by flame-like
plants, he continues to perform the traditional ritual
of expiation. Swinging the cockerel above his head, he
chants the age-old prayer recited before the Day of
Atonement, consecrating the expiatory sacrifice before
killing it. Lipchitz explained that the bearded Jew
symbolised the Jews of Europe, and that the statue
expressed his own prayer that they might be saved by
means of this sacrificial offering. Although the Jew's
blasted body suggests that the sacrifice is futile, he
contains within himself an element of hope, an innocent unborn lamb curled up in a foetal position in his
'womb'. The Jew making the sacrifice may die, but,
hopefully, he will live long enough to give birth to the
lamb who will survive him.[53]

Other artists found different methods to express
their Jewish identity. Ben Shahn, who in the 1930s
had stressed a left-wing and universalist humanitarian
approach, returned to Jewish subjects and began to
use Hebrew inscriptions as part of his reaction to the
Holocaust. William Gropper, who had been an illus-
trator for communist newspapers and had previously
mocked religious and capitalist Jews, suddenly began
in the 1940s to paint Jews in prayer and continued to

66

Col.Fig.28 Robert
Morris, *Untitled*, 1987,
silkscreen and encaustic
on aluminium panel
and painted cast
fibreglass frame,
2.57 × 3.15 m

Col.Fig.30 Mordecai Ard
Sarah, 1947, oil on board
1.38 × 1.08 m

Col.Fig.31 Friedensreich
Hundertwasser, *Blood
Garden: Houses with Yel
Smoke*, 1962 - 3, mixed
media on paper,
81 × 65 cm

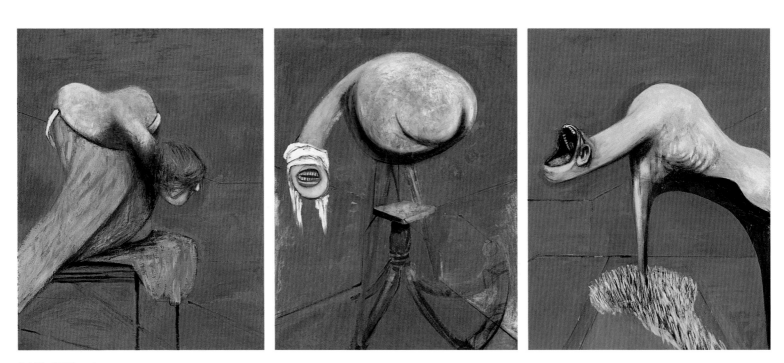

Col.Fig.32 Francis
Bacon, *Three Studies
for Figures at the Base
of a Crucifixion*,
triptych, 1944, oil and
pastel on hardboard,
each panel 94 × 74 cm

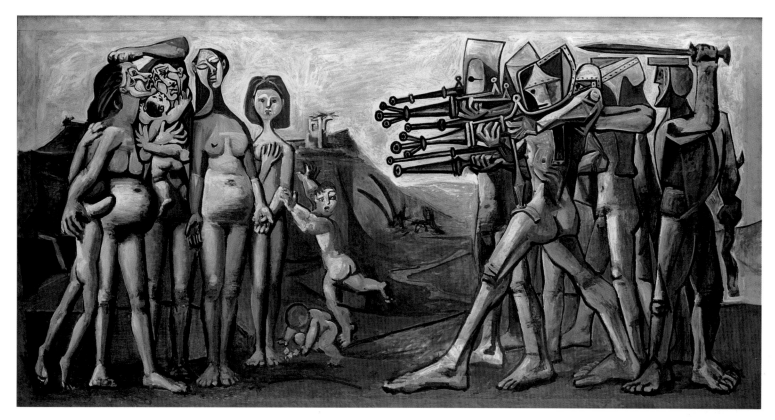

Col.Fig.33 Pablo Picasso,
Massacre in Korea, 1951,
oil on plywood, 1.10 × 2.10 m

Col.Fig.34 Zoran Music,
We Are Not the Last,
1970, acrylic on canvas,
90 × 116 cm

Fig.35 Jacques Lipchitz, *Prayer*, 1943, bronze, height 110 cm

do this at least once a year all his life. He explained that this was his form of observing the *Jahrzeit* (the traditional Jewish annual memorial for the dead) for Jews who had died in the Holocaust. After a long stay in Eastern Europe in 1948 - 50, during which he saw to what extent the Jewish communities had been devastated by the war, Gropper began to resurrect the Eastern European *shtetl* in his works, combining it with memories of his own boyhood on New York's Lower East Side.[54]

Political events in the years following the war also helped many artists to find a way of retaining their faith after the horror of the Holocaust had almost extinguished it. Both Christians and Jews saw the creation of the State of Israel not only as the positive aftermath of a tragic ordeal, but as the fulfilment of prophecies that only after a great destruction would the Jewish people return to Zion. Chagall and Lipchitz hinted at this connection by subtly changing their Holocaust motifs in response to this event. For instance, in *Liberation* of 1937 - 48, Chagall described the joy that accompanied the liberation of the camps and linked it with the creation of the State through the name he originally gave the painting, *Hatikva* (The Hope), the title of the Israeli national anthem. In like manner, Lipchitz used the imagery of his 1943 sculpture *Prayer* (Fig.35) as the basis for his *Miracle* and *Sacrifice* series of 1947 - 8 which express his prayers for the creation of the State of Israel. Through such works, artists expressed the idea that they had found some redemptive reason for the Holocaust.[55]

All these works – those dealing with Old and New Testament themes as well as those affirming Jewish faith or celebrating the creation of the State of Israel – reflect artistic attempts to explore the questions of why the Holocaust happened and who was responsible for it. The need to answer the why and wherefore of the Holocaust – both in order to understand it on an abstract level and to draw conclusions from it in order to prevent it from recurring in the future – was a major cause of artistic activity on the interpretative level. In the works we have explored so far, responsibility for the Holocaust was fixed on two levels: some artists blamed the Christian world and the Church; others blamed God. The great majority of artists, however, blamed the Nazis themselves for their murderous actions.

To convey this message, artists had to find ways to depict the Nazis in a manner that would unmask their evil. This proved difficult: artists who attempted straightforward, normal portrayals of the Nazis failed, as it was impossible to grasp how these ordinary-looking people could perpetrate such atrocities. To uncover their true character, artists followed the lead of John Heartfield's early anti-Fascist works and depicted the Nazis as predatory animals, symbols of death and human and inhuman monsters.[56] Marcel Janco, for example, in his series of drawings on the Holocaust from the war years, depicted the Nazi as a human monster who indulges in cruel mockery or exhibits terrifying rage as he tortures and kills the Jews, becoming increasingly inhuman and animal-like in the process.[57]

Towards the end of the war, however, artists and other thinkers began to ask a basic question: are cruelty and monstrosity characteristic only of the Nazis, or are they rooted in human nature?[58] Those who took the former view continued to portray the Nazi in monstrous terms, but those who embraced the latter theory began to characterise all men as monstrous – victim and perpetrator alike.[59]

One of the earliest expressions of this second view is Francis Bacon's *Three Studies for Figures at the Base of a Crucifixion* of 1944 (Col.Fig.32). Bacon created a gradual transition between the right-hand figure who symbolises the Nazi and is based on photographs of Hermann Goering, mouth wide open, making a speech, and the image of the victim on the left who bends over as he kneels with his hands tied behind his back. It is hard to identify the central figure: he is based in part on Bacon's *Figure Getting Out of a Car* of c.1939 - 40, which the artist claimed was inspired by a photograph of Hitler, but the use of a blindfold may suggest that he is a victim about to be shot.[60] Whereas the right-hand figure is the most frightening, all three are monstrous and animal-like, since in the cruel world that Bacon represents, the murderer is no more to blame than his victim. Bacon seems here to foresee Carl Jung's post-war dictum:

The wickedness of others becomes our own wickedness because it kindles something evil in our own hearts. The murder has been suffered by everyone, and everyone has committed it; lured by the irresistible fascination of evil, we have all made this collective psychic murder possible.[61]

This explanation of the painting is also borne out by Bacon's statement that the figures represent the Eumenides,[62] the Greek goddesses – more usually called the Erinyes – who punish the wrongdoer. The term Bacon chose, which means 'the kindly ones', has been explained in two ways. On the one hand, this term was used because these goddesses protect society by punishing criminals. On the other, the name is used to appease the goddesses so that they will not exact revenge. At a time when many in the Allied camp were demanding vengeance on the Nazis for their crimes against humanity, Bacon poses a more equivocal attitude. His Eumenides are both avengers, and 'kindly ones' who can be propitiated. Thus these monstrous figures are a compound of perpetrator, victim, avenger and forgiver: all share equal responsibility in a merciless and hopeless world, and the spectator is left to arrive at his own moral conclusions.[63]

This transfer of evil from the Nazis to mankind in general engendered two conflicting attitudes. One was a sense of despair at being confronted with a godless world in which the Holocaust was only one climactic example of the evil that is everywhere rampant. The other was a compulsion to appropriate Holocaust images in dealing with other contemporary problems in life and politics. Thus Picasso took the depiction of nude women and children being shot by Nazi soldiers and moved it from a Holocaust context to his *Massacre in Korea* of 1951 (Col.Fig.33), in which the women are shot by robot-like soldiers derived from Goya's *Third of May 1808*. This scene relates to no known incident in the Korean War, but is used in a politically calculated way to influence the spectator. By adapting this Holocaust image, which was still very familiar only six years after the end of the Second World War, to a new situation, Picasso established an emotional identity designed to elicit immediate and instinctive reactions: sympathy for the North Korean victims, and hatred for their American and South Korean enemies. This kind of political usage has become widespread in recent years in a number of different contexts, and raises certain problems.[64]

Everyone agrees on the importance of learning the moral lessons of the Holocaust and applying them to contemporary events in order to ensure that such a crime will not be repeated. However, the application of Holocaust imagery to entirely and inherently different situations in order to evoke an unthinking response does not really further this moral aim; it may, on the contrary, hinder it as it distorts the original meaning and lessons of the Holocaust. Moreover, the free use of these images diffuses them to the point of forgetting that the Holocaust was a singular event that occurred at a specific time to a specific people. This forgetfulness is part of a process in which the Holocaust becomes so distanced from the centre of interest as to make it possible even to deny that it ever took place.

It was a reaction against this dismissal and denial of the Holocaust that prompted Robert Morris in his series *Disappearing Places* of 1988. In these reliefs, he lowers the curtain of forgetfulness over the minor concentration camps in Poland until only half of their names remain exposed. In order to stress the meaning of the names, Morris sculpted on the curtains symbols which could be associated with the Holocaust, such as gunshot holes or the impressions left by the hands of the victims. Whereas this half-covering of the name suggests that the camps are in danger of being forgotten, the fact that half the name remains leads the

spectator to try to decipher it and to connect it with the visual image on the curtain. Thus these images of oblivion and denial actually call the Holocaust back to mind.[65]

In conclusion, despite the irresistible tension that seemingly exists between the visual arts and the Holocaust, its influence on art has been extremely pronounced. The artists had different goals: to document, to memorialise, to express a personal reaction, to understand and to draw moral lessons. Understandably, therefore, their works differed not only in terms of style and of content, but also in terms of the conclusions they drew from the Holocaust. After more than fifty years of dealing with the subject, artistic responses to the Holocaust are increasing rather than diminishing. New artists, including the children of the survivors and of the perpetrators, have begun to express themselves on this subject and to see it in new ways. Moreover, exhibitions such as the present one have been undertaken to bring these reactions uncompromisingly to the public eye. The Holocaust has become an archetype of hate and destruction, one that will probably continue to be treated in art as long as these dangers exist.

Notes

1. Jean-Paul Sartre, *Essays in Aesthetics*, trans. Wade Baskin (Citadel, New York, 1966), pp.61 - 2.
2. Theodor W. Adorno, 'Engagement', *Noten zur Literatur* 3 (Suhrkamp, Frankfurt, 1965), pp.125 - 7. For a further discussion of this problem, see Ziva Amishai-Maisels, *Depiction and Interpretation: The Influence of the Holocaust on the Visual Arts* (Pergamon, Oxford, 1993), pp.34 - 7.
3. For a discussion of the reasons behind this artistic activity and the technical difficulties of making art in the camps, see Amishai-Maisels, *Depiction and Interpretation*, pp.3 - 6; Janet Blatter and Sybil Milton, *Art of the Holocaust* (Routledge, New York, 1981), pp.24 - 35; Mary S. Costanza, *The Living Witness* (Free Press, New York, 1982), pp.21 - 46, 48 - 9, 111 - 15, 117 - 31.
4. For exceptions to this rule, including the expressionism of the Theresienstadt artists and the use of abstract art in the camps, see Amishai-Maisels, *Depiction and Interpretation*, pp.6 - 13, 248 - 9.
5. Blatter and Milton, p.142. See 'The Complexities of

Witnessing' in the present catalogue for further discussion of these issues.

6. For a discussion of the ways refugees reacted to the Holocaust, see Ziva Amishai-Maisels, 'The Artist as Refugee', in Ezra Mendelsohn (ed.) *Art and Its Uses, Studies in Contemporary Jewry* 6 (Hebrew University, Jerusalem, 1990), pp.111 - 48; and Amishai-Maisels, *Depiction and Interpretation*, pp.25 - 31, 34.

7. See Amishai-Maisels, *Depiction and Interpretation*, pp.5, 8 - 9, 11, 46 - 7, 55 - 6, 107 - 8, 118, 273, 370 n.39.

8. *Ibid.*, pp.95 - 7, 134, 138 - 9, 277 - 9, 337 - 42.

9. See the discussion of the works of the partisans and camp liberators, especially those of Corrado Cagli, *ibid.*, pp.3, 7, 13 - 14, 36 - 40, 51 - 4, 99 - 101, 104 - 7, 162, 181, 236 - 8, 384 n.70.

10. Lee Miller, 'Germans Are Like This', *Vogue* 105 (June 1945), pp.102 - 7, 192 - 3.

11. For a discussion of this problem in the 1950s which involved both artistic and other considerations, including various forms of denial, see Amishai-Maisels, *Depiction and Interpretation*, pp.66 - 73, 76 - 86, 108, 110 - 14.

12. For a discussion of this use of aesthetic models and symbols, see *ibid.*, pp.9 - 10, 14 - 21, 36 - 42, 50 - 1, 53 - 5, 63, 84, 91 - 2, 101 - 4, 108 - 10, 131 - 54.

13. For a full discussion of this subject, see *ibid.*, pp.50 - 98.

14. Michael Peppiatt, 'Zoran Music: Inspired by Dachau', *Art International*, new series 2 (Spring 1988), p.22.

15. For the reasons that led Picasso to paint this picture and contemporary testimony linking it to the Holocaust, see Amishai-Maisels, *Depiction and Interpretation*, pp.57 - 60.

16. Eg, *ibid.*, fig.172.

17. Eg, *ibid.*, figs.150 - 1.

18. London, Victoria and Albert Museum, *Exhibition of Paintings by Picasso and Matisse* (December 1945), unpaged introduction in English, corrected according to the corresponding French text.

19. For a discussion of these problems, see Amishai-Maisels, *Depiction and Interpretation*, pp.70 - 3.

20. See, for instance, Jane Fluegel's comments in New York, Museum of Modern Art, *Pablo Picasso: A Retrospective* (1980), p.380.

21. Amishai-Maisels, *Depiction and Interpretation*, fig.214. For a fuller discussion of Baskin's hanged and dead men in a Holocaust context, see *ibid.*, pp.41 - 2, 83 - 6. For an analysis of the work of one artist who broke the ban on the direct use of Holocaust iconography in the 1950s, and the fate of his works, see the discussion of Rico Lebrun in *ibid.*, pp.61 - 6, 73.

22. Erich Steingräber, *Music: Malerei, Zeichnung, Graphik* (Bruckmann, Munich, 1978), p.xviii. See also Galerie de France, Paris, *Music: Nous ne sommes pas les derniers* (18 Dec. 1970 – 30 Jan. 1971).

23. Kassel, *Documenta 8* (12 June – 20 Sept. 1987), vol.1, pp.15, 44 - 51.

24. Letter to Gannit Ankori, 29 February 1988.

25. For a fuller discussion of Morris's Holocaust works and their context within his œuvre, see Amishai-Maisels, *Depiction and Interpretation*, pp.355 - 62.

26. See the discussion of this problem in *ibid.*, pp.13 - 14, 123 - 7, 131 - 54.

27. Karlsruhe, Badischer Kunstverein, *Widerstand statt Anpassung: Deutsche Kunst im Widerstand gegen den Faschismus 1933 - 1945*, (Elefanten, Berlin, 1980), p.111.

28. Eg *Konzentrationslager* (Graphia, Karlsbad, 1934).

29. See, for instance, Stefan Lorant, 'I Was Hitler's Prisoner', *Picture Post* 2 (4 January 1939), p.71.

30. See, for instance, the use of the gates of Auschwitz in R. B. Kitaj's *If Not, Not* of 1975 - 6 (Amishai-Maisels, *Depiction and Interpretation*, colour plate 86), which can easily be overlooked unless one is familiar with their shape, and which the artist therefore felt he had to explain (*ibid.*, p.320).

31. *George Grosz: An Autobiography*, trans. Nora Hodges (Macmillan, New York, 1983), pp.292 - 6; George Grosz, *Briefe 1913 - 1959* (Rowohlt, Reinbek, 1979), pp.232, 244, 253, 259 - 62.

32. For other examples, see Amishai-Maisels, *Depiction and Interpretation*, pp.14 - 17, 109; colour plates 4, 58; figs 35 - 7, 39, 227, 282.

33. See *ibid.*, pp.131 - 4; colour plate 3; figs. 5, 34, 275, 288 - 9, 306 - 8, 311.

34. See *ibid.*, pp.132 - 3, fig.309.

35. See *ibid.*, pp.281 - 3, 348; colour plates 76 - 7, 94; figs.493 - 4, 546, 548.

36. For discussions of these subjects, see *ibid.*, pp.32 - 4, 42 - 4, 148, 151, 162, 247, 259 - 61, 321, 330, 346, 424 n.164; colour plates 67 - 8, 87, 91; figs.102, 135 - 9, 364, 547 (cattle-cars and railroad lines); pp.106 - 21, 153, 159, 165, 228 - 9, 231, 274, 300, 329; colour plates 14, 53 - 5; figs.83, 252, 272 - 89, 296, 298, 300, 368 - 9, 371 - 2, 453 - 4, 487, 530 (skeletally thin survivors); pp.4, 13 - 14, 20 - 1, 23 - 6, 28, 33 - 4, 37 - 40, 44 - 7, 51, 56, 58 - 60, 74 - 9, 85, 92, 99, 102 - 3, 108, 124 - 5, 131, 140 - 7, 162, 167 - 72, 197, 214, 231 - 5, 252, 254 - 5, 258, 261, 284, 298, 301, 316, 319, 321 - 2, 330 - 1, 340; colour plates 1, 6 - 9, 11, 14, 16, 30 - 1, 36 - 7, 39 - 40, 55 - 6, 65, 68, 77, 88, 91; figs. 11, 13, 34, 37, 39 - 41, 47 - 50, 53 - 6, 58, 62 - 6, 68 - 70, 72, 74, 76, 78 - 82, 87, 105 - 6, 109, 111 - 12, 115, 121 - 3, 135 - 6, 138 - 9, 142 - 3, 146 - 7, 173, 197, 199 - 200, 204, 218, 224 - 6, 230, 237 - 8, 254, 259, 263, 268, 302, 308, 325 - 39, 365, 375 - 7, 379 - 80, 392, 394, 396, 412 - 13, 438 - 9, 455 - 7, 508, 528 - 9, 542 (mothers and children, alone or together). The very length of the last category indicates how widespread the usage of mothers and children is in the Holocaust context.

37. See discussion *ibid.*, pp.36 - 42, colour plates 9 - 10, figs.114, 116, 120, 123 - 4, 128 - 31.

38. For a thorough investigation of this subject, see *ibid.*, pp.44 - 9, 214, 349 - 50, 359; colour plates 11 - 12, 88; figs. 140 - 9, 438, 549, 554.

39. Lea Grundig, *B'gai Haharegah* (Ha'Aretz, Tel Aviv, 1944).

40. For other depictions of this scene, see Amishai-Maisels, *Depiction and Interpretation*, pp.44 - 9, colour plates 11 - 12, figs 140 - 8, 549.

41. For a full discussion, see *ibid.*, pp.134 - 40 and passim; colour plates 13, 27 - 9, 72, 87 - 8; figs. 108, 140, 160, 163, 294, 312 - 25, 349, 537, 542; and James E. Young, *The Texture of Memory: Holocaust Memorials and Meaning* (Yale University, New Haven, 1993), endpapers, pp.28 - 37, 96, 126, 299 - 300, 303, 332 - 4.

42. See, for instance, Amishai-Maisels, *Depiction and Interpretation*, p.420, nn.73, 83. Many neighbours of the Sha'arei Zedek hospital in Jerusalem objected to the hospital's tall chimney because it reminded them of a crematorium, and they even obtained a temporary injunction against completing it.

43. For a fuller discussion of Hundertwasser's Holocaust iconography see *ibid.*, pp.135 - 8.

44. Vivianne Barsky, '"Home Is Where the Heart Is": Jewish Themes in the Art of R. B. Kitaj', in Ezra Mendelsohn, (ed.) *Art and Its Uses, Studies in Contemporary Jewry* 6 (Hebrew University, Jerusalem, 1990), pp.176 - 7; Paul Celan, *Poems* (Persea, New York, 1980), pp.50 - 3; and Jerry Glenn, *Paul Celan* (Twayne, New York, 1973), pp.67 - 9. See also Kitaj's treatment of a naked women with a baby in her arms entering a gas chamber and turning blue from the gas, in his *Germania* (Amishai-Maisels, *Depiction and Interpretation*, p.322, colour plate 88).

45. For a discussion of these works, see Amishai-Maisels, *Depiction and Interpretation*, pp.22, 155 - 6, 211, 215, 221; colour plate 5; figs 355, 431, 441, 448.

46. *Ibid.*, pp.179 - 87; colour plates 39 - 40; figs 390 - 7.

47. Ferragil Galleries, New York, *Josef Foshko* (30 Apr. – 17 May 1945), cover.

48. See Amishai-Maisels, *Depiction and Interpretation*, pp.186 - 7, 195 - 7; colour plate 41; figs. 398, 409 - 13.

49. For biblical images which symbolise other aspects of the Holocaust, see *ibid.*, pp.155 - 64, 172 - 7.

50. *Ibid.*, pp.164 - 7, colour plate 35, figs 368 - 74.

51. For Ardon's other uses of this idea in a Holocaust context, see *ibid.*, pp.257 - 62. For a fuller discussion of the Sacrifice of Isaac in this context, see *ibid.*, pp.167 - 72, colour plate 37, figs 375 - 81.

52. *Ibid.*, pp.289 - 91, colour plate 79, figs 499 - 500.

53. *Ibid.*, pp.295 - 6.

54. *Ibid.*, pp.292 - 3, 309 - 13; colour plate 80; figs 502 - 3, 516 - 17. For other examples of these aspects, see pp.288 - 9, 291 -

309, 313 - 15; colour plates 81 - 3; figs 497 - 8, 501, 504, 511 - 15, 518 - 19.

55. *Ibid.*, pp.324 - 8; figs 506, 524 - 8.

56. For a discussion of this problem, see *ibid.*, pp.207 - 24. For the type of Heartfield models involved, see *ibid.*, figs 425, 431, 441, 448.

57. Marcel Janco, *Kay Haketz* (Am Oved, Tel Aviv, 1981); and Ein Hod, Janco-Dada Museum, *Marcel Janco: On the Edge, Drawings of the Holocaust* (19 Apr. – 7 July, 1990).

58. For a later example of this line of thinking, see the quotation from Music in the text above.

59. For a discussion of the ramifications of this problem, see Amishai-Maisels, *Depiction and Interpretation*, pp.225 - 42.

60. For a discussion of the various theories on the sources for these figures, see *ibid.*, pp.190, 440 nn.126 - 8, 130.

61. C.G. Jung, 'After the Catastrophe', *Civilisation in Transition* (Pantheon, London, 1964), pp.198 - 9.

62. David Sylvester, *Francis Bacon* (Pantheon, New York, 1975), p.112.

63. For a fuller discussion of Bacon's reactions to the Holocaust, see Amishai-Maisels, *Depiction and Interpretation*, pp.189 - 91, 195 - 6, 225 - 7.

64. For other examples of Holocaust imagery used in other political contexts, see *ibid.*, pp.344 - 62.

65. *Ibid.*, p.362, fig.556.

James E. Young

Memory and Counter-Memory: Towards a Social Aesthetic of Holocaust Memorials[1]

Introduction

In keeping with the bookish, iconoclastic side of Jewish tradition, the first 'memorials' to the Holocaust period came not in stone, glass or steel – but in narrative. The Yizkor Bucher – memorial books – recalled both the lives and the destruction of European Jewish communities according to the most ancient of Jewish memorial media: the book. Indeed, as the preface to one of these books suggests, 'Whenever we pick up the book we will feel we are standing next to [the victims'] grave, because even that the murderers denied them.[2] The *shtetl* scribes hoped that when read, the Yizkor Bucher would turn the site of reading into memorial space. In response to what has been called 'the missing gravestone syndrome', the first sites of memory created by survivors were thus interior spaces, imagined gravesites.

Without realising it, perhaps, conceptual artist Jochen Gerz has recently recapitulated not only this missing gravestone syndrome but also the notion of the memorial as an interior space. I refer not to his and Esther Shalev-Gerz's vanishing monument in Harburg, discussed later in this essay, but to his more recently dedicated, invisible monument in Saarbrücken, which takes the counter-monument to, shall we say, new depths.[3]

Celebrated in Germany for his hand in Harburg's disappearing monument against Fascism, in 1991 Gerz was appointed guest professor at the School of Fine Arts in Saarbrücken. In a studio class he devoted to conceptual monuments, Gerz invited his students to participate in a clandestine memory-project, a kind of guerrilla memorial action. The class agreed enthusiastically, swore themselves to secrecy, and listened as Gerz described his plan: under the cover of night, eight students would steal into the great cobblestone square leading to the Saarbrücken *Schloss*, former home of the Gestapo during Hitler's Reich. Carrying book bags laden with cobblestones removed from other parts of the city, the students would spread themselves across the square, sit in pairs, swill beer, and yell at each other in raucous voices, pretending to have a party. All the while, in fact, they would stealthily pry loose some seventy cobblestones from the square and replace them with the similarly sized stones they had brought along, each embedded underneath with a nail so that they could be located later with a metal detector. Within days, this part of the memorial mission had been accomplished as planned.

Meanwhile, other members of the class had been assigned to research the names and locations of every former Jewish cemetery in Germany, over 2000 of them, now abandoned or vanished. When their classmates returned from the beer-party, their bags heavy with cobblestones, all set to work engraving the names of missing Jewish cemeteries on the stones, one by one. The night after they finished, the memory-guerrillas returned the stones to their original places, each inscribed and dated. But in a twist wholly consistent with the Gerzes' previous counter-monument, the stones were replaced face down, leaving no trace of the entire operation. The memorial would be invisible, itself only a memory, out of sight and therefore, Gerz hoped, *in mind*.

But as Gerz also realised, because the memorial was no longer visible, public memory would depend on knowledge of the memorial-action becoming public. Towards this end, Gerz wrote to Oskar Lafontaine, then Minister-president of the Saarland and Vice-president of the German Social Democratic Party, apprising him of the deed and asking him for parliamentary assistance to continue the operation. Lafontaine responded with 10,000 DM from a special arts fund and a warning that the entire project was patently illegal. The public, however, had now become part of the memorial. For once the newspapers got wind of the project, a tremendous furore broke out over the reported vandalisation of the square; editorials asked whether yet another monument like this was necessary; some even wondered whether or not the whole thing had been a conceptual hoax designed merely to provoke a memorial storm.

Fig.36 Jochen Gerz's *2146 Stones: A Monument Against Racism* at the *Schloss* in Saarbrücken, Germany. After inscribing each cobblestone with the name of a Jewish cemetery in Germany destroyed by the Nazis, Gerz and his students replaced the stones, inscribed-side down. The *Platz* has since been re-named 'Square of the Invisible Monument'

As visitors flocked to the square looking for the seventy stones out of over 8000, they too began to wonder 'where they stood' vis-à-vis the memorial. Were they standing on it? In it? Was it really there at all? On searching for memory, Gerz hoped, they would realise that such memory was already in them. This would be an interior memorial: as the only standing forms in the square, the visitors would become the memorials for which they searched.

Where the politicians stood was less equivocal. As Jochen Gerz rose to address the Saarbrücken Stadtverband to explain his project, the entire CDU contingent stood up and walked out. The rest of the parliament remained and voted the memorial into public existence. Indeed, they even voted to rename the plaza 'Square of the Invisible Monument', its name becoming the only visible sign of the memorial itself. Whether or not the operation had ever really taken place, the power of suggestion had already planted the memorial where it would do the most good: not in the centre of town, but in the centre of the public's mind. In effect, Jochen Gerz's *2146 Stones: A Monument Against Racism* (Fig.36 and Col.Fig.52) returns the burden of memory to those who come looking for it.

After such 'anti-monuments', neither the idea of the public monument nor the visitors' approach to it can ever be quite the same. As contemporary monument-makers continue to challenge the very idea of the monument, to enliven the monument with the sense of its changes over time, we who visit these monuments might begin to rethink our own relationship to them and the memory they would embody. Rather than merely surveying these memorials in the pages that follow, therefore, or attempting to cull 'good' monuments from 'bad', I would like to explore a 'social-aesthetic' of Holocaust memorials that takes into account the monument's essentially social life in the public eye. For in fact, it may be precisely the public's interaction with the monument that finally constitutes its aesthetic life. This is to suggest that the 'art

of public memory' encompasses not just these memorials' aesthetic contours, or their place in contemporary artistic discourse. It also includes the activity that brought them into being, the constant give and take between memorials and viewers, and finally, the responses of viewers to their own world in light of a memorialised past – the consequences of memory.

The Monument in Historical Context

The further events of the Second World War recede into time, the more prominent its memorials become. As the period of the Holocaust is shaped in the survivors' diaries and memoirs, in their children's films and novels and artworks, public memory of this time is being moulded in a proliferating number of memorial images and spaces. Depending on where these memorials are constructed and by whom, these sites remember the past according to a variety of national myths, ideals and political needs. Some recall war dead, others resistance, and still others mass murder. All reflect both the past experiences and current lives of their communities, as well as the State's memory of itself. At a more specific level, these memorials also reflect the temper of the memory-artists' time, their place in aesthetic discourse, their media and materials.

Memory is never shaped in a vacuum, the motives of memory are never pure. The reasons given for Holocaust memorials and the kinds of memory they generate are as various as the sites themselves. Some are built in response to traditional Jewish injunctions to remember, others according to a government's need to explain a nation's past to itself. Where the aim of some memorials is to educate the next generation and to inculcate in it a sense of shared experience and destiny, other memorials are conceived as expiations of guilt or as self-aggrandisement. Still others are intended to attract tourists. In addition to traditional Jewish memorial iconography, every State has its own institutional forms of remembrance. As a result, Holocaust memorials inevitably mix national and Jewish figures, political and religious imagery.

In Germany, for example, memorials to this time recall Jews by their absence, non-Jewish German victims by their political resistance. In Poland, countless memorials in former death camps and across the countryside commemorate the whole of Polish destruction through the figure of its murdered Jewish part. In Israel, martyrs and heroes are remembered side-by-side, both redeemed by the birth of the State. Just as the shape Holocaust memory takes in Europe and Israel is determined by political, aesthetic and religious coordinates, that in America is guided no less by distinctly American ideals and experiences – such as liberty, pluralism and immigration.

By themselves, these monuments are of little value, mere stones in the landscape. But as part of a nation's rites or the objects of a people's national pilgrimage, they are invested with national soul and memory. For traditionally, the State-sponsored memory of a national past aims to affirm the righteousness of a nation's birth, even its divine election. The matrix of a nation's monuments emplots the story of ennobling events, of triumphs over barbarism, and recalls the martyrdom of those who gave their lives in the struggle for national existence – who, in the martyrological

Fig.37 Monument at the Majdanek death camp near Lublin, Poland, designed by Wikto Tolkin, 1969. Through its abstraction, a large form perched on relatively undersized bases, the sculptor has attempted to suggest an ominous sense of danger to those standing beneath it

refrain, died so that a country might live. In assuming the idealised forms and meanings assigned this era by the State, memorials tend to concretise particular historical interpretations. They suggest themselves as indigenous, even geological outcroppings in a national landscape; in time, such idealised memory grows as natural to the eye as the landscape in which it stands. Indeed, for memorials to do otherwise would be to undermine the very foundations of national legitimacy, of the State's seemingly natural right to exist.

The relationship between a State and its memorials is not, however, one-sided. On the one hand, official agencies are in the position to shape memory explicitly as they see fit, memory that best serves a national interest. On the other hand, once created, memorials take on lives of their own, often stubbornly resistant to the State's original intentions. In some cases, memorials created in the image of a State's ideals actually turn around to recast these ideals in the memorial's own image. New generations visit memorials under new circumstances and invest them with new meanings. The result is an evolution in the memorial's significance, generated in the new times and company in which it finds itself.

Over the course of the last century, in fact, the very idea of the memorial-monument and its place in modern culture has generated as much dissension as unity. Indeed, the traditional assumption of the monument's timelessness has nearly relegated it as a form to the margins of modern discourse. For once it was recognised that monuments necessarily mediate memory, even as they seek to inspire it, they came to be regarded as displacements of the memory they were supposed to embody. Even worse, by insisting that its memory was as fixed as its place in the landscape, the monument seemed to ignore the essential mutability in all cultural artifacts. 'What is the use to the modern man of this "monumental" contemplation of the past', Nietzsche asked. 'Monumental history' was, after all, Nietzsche's disdainful epithet for any version

of history calling itself permanent and everlasting, a petrified history that buried the living.[4]

A few years later, Lewis Mumford echoed Nietzsche's scorn for the monumental when he pronounced the death of the monument in its hopeless incompatibility with his sense of modern architectural forms. 'The notion of a modern monument is veritably a contradiction in terms,' he wrote. '[If] it is a monument, it is not modern, and if it is modern, it cannot be a monument.' In Mumford's view, the monument defied the very essence of modern urban civilisation: the capacity for renewal and rejuvenation. Where modern architecture invites the perpetuation of life itself, encourages renewal and change, and scorns the illusion of permanence, Mumford wrote, 'Stone gives a false sense of continuity, and a deceptive assurance of life'.

Instead of changing and adapting to its environment, the monument remained static, a mummification of ancient, probably forgotten ideals. Instead of placing their faith in the powers of biological regeneration, fixing their images in their children, the eminent and powerful had traditionally sought in their vanity a petrified immortality. In Mumford's words, 'They write their boasts upon tombstones; they incorporate their deeds in obelisks; they place their hopes of remembrance in solid stones joined to other solid stones, dedicated to their subjects or their heirs forever, forgetful of the fact that stones that are deserted by the living are even more helpless than life that remains unprotected and preserved by stones'.[5] Indeed, after his mentor Patrick Geddes, Mumford suggests that it was usually the shakiest of regimes that installed the least movable monuments, a compensation for having accomplished nothing worthier by which to be remembered.

More recently, the late German historian, Martin Broszat, has suggested that in their references to the Fascist era, monuments may not remember events so much as bury them altogether beneath layers of national myths and explanations.[6] As cultural reifications, in this view, monuments reduce or, in Broszat's

words, 'coarsen' historical understanding as much as they generate it. In another vein, art historian Rosalind Krauss finds that the modernist period produces monuments unable to refer to anything beyond themselves as pure marker or base.[7] After Krauss, we might ask, in fact, whether an abstract, self-referential monument can ever commemorate events outside of itself. Or must it motion endlessly to its own gesture to the past, a commemoration of its essence as dislocated sign, forever trying to remember events it never actually knew?

Still others have argued that rather than embodying memory, the monument displaces it altogether, supplanting a community's memory-work with its own material form. 'The less memory is experienced from the inside,' Pierre Nora warns, 'the more it exists through its exterior scaffolding and outward signs.'[8] If the obverse of this is true as well, then perhaps the more memory comes to rest in its exteriorised forms, the less it is experienced internally. In this age of mass-memory production and consumption, in fact, the memorialisation of the past and its contemplation and study seem to be in inverse proportion. For once we assign monumental form to memory, we have to some degree divested ourselves of the obligation to remember. In shouldering the memory-work, monuments may relieve viewers of their memory burden.

Fig.38 The memorial at Treblinka, designed by Adam Haupt and Franciszek Duszenko and dedicated in 1964, consists of 17,000 granite shards set in concrete around a 26-foot-high obelisk. It is meant to recall the greatest of all genocidal cemeteries

Added to this is a contemporary scepticism about the supposedly common values we all bring to public spaces, one of the reasons for the uprising against so much public art. 'In the absence of shared belief and even common interests,' John Hallmark Neff writes, 'it should not be surprising that so much of the well-intentioned art acquired for public spaces has failed – failed as art and as art for a civic site.'[9] That is, Neff suggests, without a set of shared expectations, beliefs or interests, artists and their prospective public audience have no grounds for engagement, no common cultural language in which they might even argue their respective views.

But this formulation may overlook one of the basic functions of all 'public art': the very creation of shared spaces that would lend a common spatial frame to otherwise disparate experiences and understanding. Rather than presuming a common set of ideals, the public monument attempts to create an architectonic ideal by which even competing memories might be figured. In this light, Neff's observation might be modified: in the absence of shared beliefs or common interests, art in public spaces may force an otherwise fragmented populace to frame diverse values and ideals in common spaces. By creating common spaces for memory, monuments propagate the illusion of common memory.

As is clear by any State's official use of commemorative spaces, this function of monuments is clear most of all to the governments themselves. Though the utopian vision may hold that monuments are unnecessary as reminders when all can remember for themselves, Maurice Halbwachs argued persuasively that it is primarily through membership in religious, national or class groups that people are able to acquire and then recall their memories at all.[10] That is, both the reasons for memory and the forms memory takes are always socially-mandated, part of a socialising system whereby fellow-citizens gain common history through the vicarious memory of their forbears' experiences. If part of the State's aim, therefore, is to create a sense

of shared values and ideals, then it will also be the State's aim to create the sense of common memory, as foundation for a unified city-state. Public memorials, national days of commemoration, and shared calendars thus all work to create common loci around which national identity is forged.

To the extent that all societies depend on the assumption of shared experience and memory for the very basis of their common relations, a society's institutions are automatically geared towards creating a shared memory – or at least the illusion of it. By creating the sense of a shared past, such institutions as national memorial days, for example, foster the sense of a common present and future, even a sense of shared national destiny. In this way, memorials provide the sites where groups of people gather to create a common past for themselves, places where they tell the constitutive narratives, their 'shared' stories of the past. They become communities precisely by having shared (if only vicariously) the experiences of their neighbours. At some point, it may even be the activity of remembering together that becomes the shared memory; once ritualised, remembering together becomes an event in itself shared, itself to be remembered.

In addition to national context, a monument's topographical environment also works to generate very specific meaning in memory. For a monument necessarily transforms an otherwise benign site into part of its content, even as it is absorbed into the site and made part of a larger locale. In this way, a monument becomes a point of reference amid other parts of the landscape, one node among others in a topographical matrix that orients the rememberer and creates symbolic meaning in both the land and our recollections. Moreover, where European memorials located *in situ* often suggest themselves rhetorically as the extension of events they would commemorate, those removed from the 'topography of terror' tend inevitably to call attention to the great distance between themselves and the destruction.

In this sense, American Holocaust memorials seem

Fig.39 Hans Haacke's 'point of reference' after it was firebombed by Neo-Nazis, 2 November 1988

not to be anchored in history so much as in the ideals that generated them in the first place. The US Holocaust Memorial Museum, for example, necessarily resonates to other nearby national monuments, recalling the Holocaust as counterpoint to American democratic and egalitarian ideals. Likewise, the 'Liberation' monument in New Jersey's Liberty Park forms part of an immigrant triad, with Ellis Island and the Statue of Liberty in sight. A new Holocaust memorial in Boston will derive further American meaning from its place on the 'Freedom Trail', integrating the Holocaust into the very myth of American origins.

The Aesthetic Interrogation of the Monument

In every case, Holocaust memorials reflect not only national and communal remembrance, or their geographical locations, but also the memorial designer's own time and place. For contemporary artists working in decidedly unmonumental media, the 'art of the monument' cuts at least two ways. On the one hand, when invited to conceive of a Holocaust memorial, contemporary artists turn reflexively to their chosen medium, style and forms. For like their generational counterparts in literature and music, most of the contemporary artists commissioned to design memorials remain answerable to both art and memory. In a hypothetical marker they designed for the Anne Frank House in Amsterdam, for example, Doug and Mike Starn have overlaid sepia-tinted automat photographs of Anne onto an enlarged page of her *Diary*. Instead of segmenting these photographs, they have left them in two series of three intact, paired side-by-side, almost twin-like. The *Diary* page, her last, is dated and so recalls the dates of a tombstone, her epitaph self-inscribed.

Hans Haacke, as he has done so effectively with the icons of big business, resurrected a Nazi memorial in Graz, Austria in order to remind all of the site's complicitous past. In 'Bezugspunkte 38/88' [Points of Reference 38/88], a city-wide installation, the artist duplicated the Nazis' draping of the town's patron saint in swastika-emblazoned banners in order to turn the image of Nazism against itself.[11] Haacke's 'point of reference' was itself turned inside out when neo-Nazis torched the monument, an act which the artist then incorporated into the text of the memorial by adding the inscription: 'On the night of 9 November 1938, all synagogues in Austria were looted, destroyed, and set on fire. And during the night of 2 November 1988, this memorial was destroyed by a firebomb.' (See Fig.39)[12]

In a work entitled *Altar to the Chajes High School* Christian Boltanski has likewise extended his earlier work, mixing fuzzy photographs, lightbulbs and wires to recall a Jewish day school, the instruments of memory, and the resulting difficulty of memory. Sol LeWitt's black cube set in the square of a former palace in Munster (Fig.40) recalled both the absent Jews of Munster and his own geometrical forms – before the monument itself was dismantled by town authorities (and later rebuilt in Hamburg-Altona). When commissioned to create a monument for San Francisco, George Segal turned automatically to the plaster-white figures of his earlier work, using an Israeli survivor as his primary model (Col.Fig.51). In fact, as Albert Elsen reminds us, for many contemporary artists, it will be the needs of art, not the public or memory, that come first.[13]

At the same time, a new generation of artists in Germany has begun to wonder whether the monument itself is more an impediment than an incitement to public memory. Ethically certain of their duty to remember, but aesthetically sceptical of the assumptions underpinning traditional memorial forms, a new generation of contemporary artists and monument-makers in Germany is probing the limits of both their artistic media and the very notion of a memorial. Indeed, for many of these artists, the Holocaust monument has come to embody Germany's fundamental memorial dilemma: how does a country like Germany build a new and just State on the bedrock memory of its terrible crimes? How does a nation remember events it would rather forget?

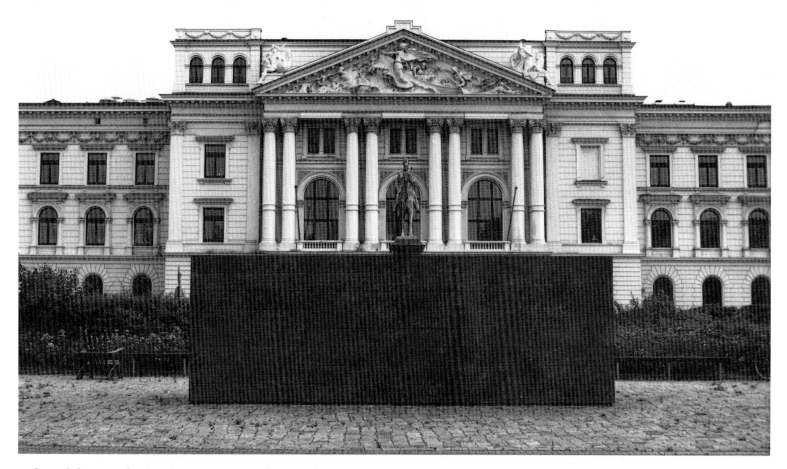

Fig.40 Sol LeWitt's *Black Form* in its new home in front of the Town Hall in Hamburg-Altona, 1989

One of the most fascinating responses to Germany's memorial conundrum is the rise of its 'counter-monuments': brazen, painfully self-conscious memorial spaces conceived to challenge the very premises of their being. For these artists are heirs to a double-edged post-war legacy: a deep distrust of monumental forms in light of their systematic exploitation by the Nazis and a profound desire to distinguish their generation from that of the killers through memory.[11] To their minds, the didactic logic of monuments, their demagogical rigidity, recall too closely traits they associate with Fascism itself. A monument against Fascism, therefore, would have to be a monument against itself: against the traditionally didactic function of monuments, against their tendency to displace the past they would have us contemplate – and finally, against the authoritarian propensity in all art that reduces viewers to passive spectators.

For German artists and sculptors like Jochen Gerz, Norbert Radermacher, Horst Hoheisel and Hans Haacke, as well as American artists and architects working in Germany, such as Sol LeWitt, Daniel Libeskind and Shimon Attie, the possibility that memory of events so grave might be reduced to exhibitions of public craftsmanship or cheap pathos remains intolerable. They contemptuously reject the traditional forms and reasons for public memorial art, those spaces that either console viewers or redeem such tragic events, or indulge in a facile kind of *Wiedergutmachung* or purport to mend the memory of a murdered people. Instead of searing memory into public consciousness, they fear, conventional memorials seal memory off from awareness altogether. These artists fear rightly that to the extent that we encourage monuments to do our memory-work for us, we become that much more forgetful. They believe, in effect, that the initial impulse to memorialise events like the Holocaust may actually spring from an opposite and equal desire to forget them.

Fig.41 Harburg's 'Monument against Fascism', designed by Jochen Gerz and Esther Shalev-Gerz, shortly after its unveiling in 1986, before its first sinking

How does the monument interrogate itself? Jochen Gerz and Esther Shalev-Gerz designed a 12-metre-tall lead-covered column in Harburg, Germany that invited visitors to inscribe their names on it (Fig.41). As sections of their 'Monument against Fascism' were covered with memorial graffiti, the column was sunk into the ground over a span of seven years (Fig.42). For the artists, the spectacle of Germans burying their anti-Fascist monument seemed to exemplify Germany's national memorial ambivalence. How better to remember a vanished people than by an ever-vanishing monument? How better to remark an absence than by creating a monument that feeds on its own absence? In the end, the artists hoped, the vanishing monument will have returned the burden of memory to visitors: the only things left standing here

Fig.42 Harburg's vanishing 'Monument against Fascism', almost gone

Fig.43 The negative-form monument to the Aschrott-Brunnen (1987), phantom-like in its whiteness, shown here before being inverted and lowered into the ground

Fig.44 At Horst Hoheisel's negative-form monument to the Aschrott-Brunnen in Kassel, the visitor is the monument

now are the memory-tourists, forced to rise and remember for themselves.

In a similar vein, artist Horst Hoheisel designed a 'negative-form' monument in Kassel, a replication of a destroyed Jewish-sponsored monument built into the ground instead of above it, which forces visitors to shoulder memory themselves, to become, in essence, the monument (Figs 43 and 44). Yet other recent works also capture the essential ambivalence of German memory, the ways that sites depend on people for their memory. Thus would slide projections by Shimon Attie (see Col.Fig.55) and Norbert Radermacher bathe otherwise forgetful sites in Berlin with images and narratives of their recent pasts. Once challenged in these ways, the idea of the monument – Holocaust or otherwise – will never be quite the same.[15]

In fact, as many contemporary artists have long recognised, the process of the memorial competition itself is often at least as rewarding as the final result. For Holocaust memory is always 'contested' as long as more than one group or individual remembers. Not only does an open memorial competition make such competing memories palpable, but it also throws into relief the complex, nearly impossible questions facing every artist or architect attempting to conceive of such a monument. Among the dilemmas for contemporary Holocaust monument makers are: how to remember horribly real events in the abstract gestures of geometric forms? How to create a focal point for remembrance among ruins without desecrating the space itself? How to embody remembrance without seeming to displace it?

These questions and others arose with the very first open competition for a memorial at Auschwitz-Birkenau in 1957 – and tend to repeat themselves in all subsequent contests. 'The choice of a monument to commemorate Auschwitz has not been an easy task,' the sculptor Henry Moore wrote as head of the internationally acclaimed design jury assembled for the Auschwitz competition. 'Essentially, what has been

attempted here has been the creation – or, in the case of the jury, the choice – of a monument to crime and ugliness, to murder and to horror. The crime was of such stupendous proportions that any work of art must be on an appropriate scale. But apart from this, is it in fact possible to create a work of art that can express the emotions engendered by Auschwitz?'[16]

In Moore's opinion, a very great sculptor – a Michelangelo or Rodin – might have been up to the task. As for the 426 submissions his jury reviewed, however, none was fully satisfactory. Many of the works were brilliant, Moore conceded, but none satisfied the criteria of all the jury, which included artists, architects, critics and – the most critical judges of all – survivors. For artists working in the period of abstract expressionism, earthworks and conceptual art, and for architects answerable to post-modern and deconstructivist design, their public is clear. Artists, critics and curators generally applaud such designs – and run up immediately against a wall of survivors' outrage. For survivors, the searing reality of their experiences demands as literal and figurative a memorial expression as possible. 'We weren't tortured and our families weren't murdered in the abstract,' survivors complain. Or in the words of Nathan Rapoport, designer of the Warsaw Ghetto Memorial, who once asked plaintively, 'Could I have made a rock with a hole in it and said "Voilà! The heroism of the Jews?"'

Probably not. All of which raises the dual roles of public and memory in public art: for as becomes clear, not every work of public art is a monument, not every memorial a work of public art. Instead of being paralysed by the tug and pull of so many competing constituencies, Henry Moore's jury finally decided to compromise. They chose what they judged to be the three strongest teams and asked them to collaborate on one final submission, either taking the best parts of their separate submissions or arriving at a new design altogether. The result, a composite, was finally unveiled at the end of the railroad tracks at Auschwitz-Birkenau in 1967 (Figs 45 and 46).

Fig.45 Memorial as it was realised at Birkenau. Between 1967 and 1989, the tablets read in eighteen different languages, 'four million people suffered and died here at the hands of the Nazi murderers, 1940 - 1945'

Although not a Holocaust memorial, Richard Serra's *Tilted Arc* and its removal from the government plaza in New York further illustrates the dilemma facing contemporary Holocaust monument-makers. On the one hand, *Tilted Arc* was scrupulously true to its maker's vision, his material, his time and place: a 12-foot-high, rusted steel wall cutting across Federal Plaza in Lower Manhattan. At the same time, however, it was precisely the work's integrity and brilliance that alienated the very public for which it was

intended. *Tilted Arc* could not have it both ways: it could not please a community of artists who almost unanimously supported it and lay-viewers disturbed by what they perceived as a violation of their public space. The conundrum remains: how is the artist going to be answerable both to his discourse and to public taste at the same time? How is he or she to balance the needs of a lay-public against the occasionally obscure sensibilities of contemporary art – all of which may depend on civic administrative approval?

Fig.46 The memorial tablets at Birkenau, swept clean of inscriptions by the post-communist regime, await new memory

Nor is this dilemma particularly new. For as Elsen has also noted, modern and avant-garde sculptors between the wars in Europe were rarely invited to commemorate either the victories or losses, battles or war-dead of the First World War.[17] The reluctance on the part of donors and government sponsors to commission abstract memorials, in particular, seems to have stemmed from two parallel impulses in the public and State. On the one hand, the aim of war-related memorials was perceived generally to valorise the suffering in such a way as to justify it historically. On the other hand, this aim was best accomplished by recalling traditional heroic icons in order to invest memory of recent war with past pride and loyalties, which would also explain that war in ways visible and seemingly self-evident to the public. In both cases, figurative imagery seemed to naturalise best the State's memorial messages. At the same time, however, it was also clear to those in a position to memorialise the First World War that the primary aim of modern sculptors after the war was to repudiate and lament – not affirm – both the historical realities and the archaic values seeming to have spawned them.

Not that many of the modern sculptors would have shown much interest in such projects to begin with. In 1918, at the end of what was regarded as the nadir of European civilisation, artists and monument-makers vociferously resisted traditional mimetic and heroic evocations of events, contending that any such remembrance would elevate and mythologise events. In their view, yet another classically proportioned Prometheus would have falsely glorified and thereby affirmed the horrible suffering they were called upon to commemorate. In the minds of many graphic and literary artists of the time, this would have been tantamount to betraying not only their experience of the Great War, but also the new reasons for art's existence after the war: to challenge the world's realities and the conventions encouraging them. If figurative statuary were demanded of them, then only anti-heroic figures would do, as exemplified in the pathetic heroes of Wilhelm Lehmbruck's *Fallen Man* and *Seated Youth* (1917). As true to the artists' inter-war vision as these works may have been, however, neither public nor State seemed ready to abide memorial edifices built on foundations of doubt instead of valour. The pathetic hero was thus condemned by emerging totalitarian regimes in Germany and Russia as defeatist for seeming to embody all that was worth forgetting – not remembering – in the war.

In addition to the ways abstraction was thought to ameliorate a work's sense of mimetic witness, it also seemed to frustrate the memorial's capacity as locus for shared self-image and commonly held ideals. In its hermetic and personal vision, abstraction encourages private visions in viewers, which would defeat the communal and collective aims of public memorials. On the one hand, the specificity of realistic figuration would seem to thwart multiple messages, while abstract sculpture could accommodate as many meanings as could be projected on to it. But in fact, it is almost always a figurative monument like the Warsaw Ghetto Memorial that serves as point of departure for political performances (see Figs 47 and 48). It is as if figurative sculpture such as this were needed to engage viewers with likenesses of people, to evoke an empathic link between viewer and monument that might then be marshalled into particular meaning.

The fundamental dilemma facing contemporary monument-makers is thus two-sided and recalls that facing prospective witnesses in any medium: first, how does one refer to events in a medium doomed to refer only to itself? And second, if the aim is to remember – *ie* to refer to – a specific person, defeat or victory, how can it be done abstractly? For many who survived to testify to the Holocaust, memory and testimony are one: witness for these survivors entails the most literal transmission possible of what they had seen and experienced. Since few artist-survivors would regard themselves as interested in form alone, as became clear in the art recovered from the ghettos and camps, even artists of the avant-garde redefined their aesthetic

Fig.47 Frontal view of the Warsaw Ghetto Monument's fighters, designed by Nathan Rapoport, 1948. The dedication reads: 'To the Jewish people – its heroes and its martyrs'

task as testimonial realists.[18] What has come to be regarded as 'documentary' art and literature seemed to them the only mode in which evidence or witness could be delivered. But as historians and literary critics have come to accept the impulse in writers to testify in narrative, even as they look beyond witness to the kinds of knowledge created in such writing, so might critical viewers of Holocaust memorials accept the parallel impulse in Holocaust memorial makers to testify through literal figuration – before turning to the ways that public memory is organised in such figures.

Towards a Social Aesthetic of Holocaust Memorials
As is clear by now, public art in general, and Holocaust memorials in particular, tend to beg traditional art-historical inquiry. Most discussions of Holocaust memorial spaces ignore the essentially public dimension of their performance, remaining either formally aestheticist or almost piously historical. So while it is true that a sculptor like Nathan Rapoport will never be regarded by art historians as highly as his contemporaries, Jacques Lipchitz and Henry Moore, neither can his work be dismissed solely on the basis of its popular appeal. Unabashedly figurative, heroic and referential, his work seems to be doomed critically by precisely those qualities – public accessibility and historical referentiality – that make it monumental. But in fact, it may be just this public appeal that finally constitutes the monument's aesthetic performance – and that leads such memorials to demand public and historical disclosure, even as they condemn themselves to critical obscurity. Instead of stopping at formal questions, or at issues of historical referentiality, we must go on to ask how memorial representations of history may finally weave themselves into the course of ongoing events.

While questions of high and low art may well continue to inform the debate surrounding Holocaust monuments, they must not dictate the critical discussion any longer. Instead, we might keep in mind the

reductive – occasionally vulgar – excesses in popular memorial representations, even as we qualify our definitions of kitsch and challenge its usefulness as a critical category for the discussion of public monuments. Rather than patronising mass tastes, we recognise the sheer weight of public taste and that certain conventional forms in avowedly public art may eventually have consequences for public memory – whether or not we think they should. This is to acknowledge the unfashionable, often archaic aspects of so many Holocaust memorials, even as we look beyond them. It is also to recognise that public art like this demands additional critical criteria if the lives and meanings of such works are to be sustained – and not oppressed – by art-historical discourse.

For there is a difference between avowedly public art – exemplified in public monuments such as these – and art produced almost exclusively for the art world, its critics, other artists, and galleries, which has yet to be properly recognised. People do not come to Holocaust memorials because they are new, 'cutting edge' or fashionable; as the critics are quick to note, most of these memorials are none of these. Where a great deal of contemporary art is produced as self- or medium-reflexive, public Holocaust monuments are produced specifically to be historically referential, to lead viewers beyond themselves to an understanding or evocation of events. As public *historical* monuments, these memorials generally avoid referring hermetically to the processes that brought them into being. Where much contemporary art invites viewers and critics to contemplate its own materiality, or its relationship to other works before and after itself, the aim of memorials is not to remark their own presence so much as past events *because* they are no longer present. In this sense, Holocaust memorials attempt to point immediately beyond themselves.

In their fusion of public art and popular culture, historical memory and political consequences, therefore, these monuments demand an alternative critique that goes beyond questions of high and low art, taste-

Fig.48 Bas-relief on the reverse side of the Warsaw Ghetto, showing Jewish martyrs

fulness and vulgarity. Rather than merely identifying the movements and forms from which public memory is born, or asking whether or not these monuments reflect past history accurately or fashionably, we turn to the many ways this art suggests itself as a basis for political and social action. That is, we might ask here not only how the monument-maker's era and training shaped memory at the time, and how the monument would reflect past history, but most important, what role it now plays in current history.

We might now concern ourselves less with whether this is good or bad art, and more with what the consequences of public memorial art are for the people. This is to propose that like any public art space, Holocaust memorials are neither benign nor irrelevant, but suggest themselves as the basis for political and communal action. With apologies to Peter Bürger, I would like to suggest here a reworking of what he has called the 'functional analysis of art', adapted to examine the social effects of public memorial spaces.[19] The aim here will be to explore not just the relations between people and their monuments but the consequences of these relations in historical time.

Whereas some art historians have traditionally dismissed such approaches to art as anthropological, social or psychological, others have opened their inquiry to include larger issues of the sociology of art: public memorials in this case are exemplary of an art work's social life, its life in society's mind. As Marianne Doezema has already suggested, there is much more to the monument's performance than its mere style, or school of design. 'The public monument,' she writes, 'has a responsibility apart from its qualities as a work of art. It is not only the private expression of an individual artist; it is also a work of art created for the public, and therefore can and should be evaluated in terms of its capacity to generate human reactions.'[20] To my mind, such reaction refers not just to an emotional effect, but to the actual consequences for people in their monuments. Not, how are people moved by these memorials? But rather, to what end have they been moved, to what historical conclusions, to what understanding and actions in their own lives? This is to suggest that we cannot separate the monument from its public life, that the social function of such art *is* its aesthetic performance.

'There is nothing in this world as invisible as a monument,' Robert Musil once wrote. 'They are no doubt erected to be seen – indeed, to attract attention. But at the same time they are impregnated with something that repels attention ...'[21] This 'something' is the essential stiffness monuments share with all other images: as a likeness necessarily vitrifies its otherwise dynamic referent, a monument turns pliant memory to stone. And it is this 'finish' that repels our attention, that makes a monument invisible. It is as if a monument's life in the communal mind grows as hard and polished as its exterior form, its significance as fixed as its place in the landscape. For monuments at rest like this – in stasis – seem to present themselves as eternal parts of the landscape, as naturally arranged as nearby trees or rock formations.

As an inert piece of stone, the monument keeps its own past a tightly held secret, gesturing away from its own history to the events and meanings we bring to it in our visits. Precisely because monuments seem to remember everything but their own past, their own creation, our critical aim here will now be to reinvest the monument with our memory of its coming into being. None of this is intended to fix the monument's meaning in time, which would effectively embalm it. Instead, I hope to reinvigorate these monuments with the memory of their acquired pasts, to vivify memory of events by writing into them our memory of the monument's origins.

By returning to the memorial some memory of its own genesis, we remind ourselves of the memorial's essential fragility, its dependence on others for its life; that it was made by human hands in human times and places, that it is no more a natural piece of the landscape than we are. For unlike words on a page, memorial icons seem to embody ideas, inviting viewers to mistake material presence and weight for immutable permanence. If, in its glazed exteriority, we never really see the monument, I would attempt here to crack its eidetic veneer, to loosen meaning, to make visible the activity of memory in monuments. It is my hope that a critique may save our *icons* of remembrance from hardening into *idols* of remembrance.[22]

All of which is meant to expand the texts of these memorials to include not only their conception and execution among historical realities, but also their current and changing lives, even their eventual destruction. This is to draw back into view the very process, the many complicated historical, political and aesthetic axes, on which memory is being constructed. For neither memory nor intention is ever monolithic: each depends on the vast array of forces – material, aesthetic, spatial, ideological – converging in one memorial site. By reinvesting these memorials with the memory of their origins, I hope to highlight the process of public art over its often static result, the ever-changing life of the monument over its seemingly frozen face in the landscape.[23]

For too often, a community's monuments assume the polished, finished veneer of a death mask, unreflective of current memory, unresponsive to contemporary issues. Instead of embodying an already enshrined memory, such an approach might provide a uniquely instructive glimpse of the monument's inner-life – the tempestuous social, political and aesthetic forces – normally hidden by a monument's taciturn exterior. By drawing back into view the memorial-making process, we invigorate the very idea of the monument, thereby reminding all such cultural artifacts of their coming into being, their essential constructedness.

To this end, I enlarge the life and texture of Holocaust memorials to include: the times and places in which they were conceived; their literal construction amid historical and political realities; their finished forms in public spaces; their places in the constellation of national memory; and their ever-evolving lives in the minds of their communities and of the Jewish people over time. With these dimensions in mind, we look not only at the ways individual monuments create and reinforce particular memory of the Holocaust period, but also at the ways events re-enter political life shaped by monuments.

On a more general level, we might ask of all memorials what meanings are generated when the temporal realm is converted to material form, when time collapses into space, a trope by which it is then measured

Fig.49 A Polish woman contemplates the broken-tombstone monument to the murdered Jews of Kazimierz-Dolny, designed by Tadeusz Augustynek, 1984

and grasped. How do memorials emplot time and memory? How do they impose borders on time, a façade on memory? What is the relationship of time to place, place to memory, memory to time? Finally, two fundamentally inter-related questions: how does a particular place shape our memory of a particular time? And how does this memory of a past time shape our understanding of the present moment?

In such questions, we also recognise the integral part visitors play in the memorial text: how and what we remember in the company of a monument depends very much on who we are, why we care to remember and how we see. When elsewhere I incorporate other visitors' responses into my descriptions of monuments, I acknowledge that in my sharing the memorial space with them, their responses become part of my experience, part of the total memorial text. All of which is to suggest the fundamentally interactive, dialogical quality of every memorial space. For public memory and its meanings depend not just on the forms and figures in the monument itself, but on the viewers' response to the monument, how it is used politically and religiously in the community, who sees it under what circumstances, how its figures enter other media and are recast in new surroundings.

Through this attention to the activity of memorialisation, we might also remind ourselves that public memory is constructed, that understanding of events depends on memory's construction, and that there are worldly consequences in the kinds of historical understanding generated by monuments. In this light, we find that the performance of Holocaust memorials depends not on some measured distance between history and its monumental representations, but in the conflation of private and public memory, in the memorial activity by which minds reflecting on the past inevitably precipitate in the present historical moment.

It is not enough to ask whether or not our memorials remember the Holocaust, or even how they remember it. We should also ask to what ends we have

remembered. That is, how do we respond to the current moment in the light of our remembered past? This is to recognise that the shape of memory cannot be divorced from the actions taken in its behalf, and that memory without consequences contains the seeds of its own destruction. For were we passively to remark only the contours of these memorials, were we to leave unexplored their genesis, and remain unchanged by the recollective act, it could be said that we have not remembered at all.

Notes

1. This essay has been adapted from the author's full-length study, *The Texture of Memory: Holocaust Memorials and Meaning* (Yale University Press, New Haven and London, 1993).
2. From 'Forwort', in *Sefer Yizkor le-kedoshei ir (Przedecz) Pshaytask Khurbanot ha'shoah*, p.130, as quoted in Jack Kugelmass and Jonathan Boyarin, eds, *From a Ruined Garden: The Memorial Books of Polish Jewry* (Schocken Books, New York, 1983), p.11.
3. For an extended discussion of German counter-monuments, see James E. Young, 'The Counter-monument: Memory against Itself in Germany Today', *Critical Inquiry* 18 (Winter 1992) pp.267-96. Also see *The Texture of Memory*, pp.17-48.
4. Friedrich Nietzsche, *The Use and Abuse of History*, trans. Adrian Collins (Macmillan Publishing Company, New York, 1985), pp.14-17.
5. Lewis Mumford, *The Culture of Cities* (Harcourt, Brace, Jovanovich, New York, 1938), pp.434 and 438.
6. For the full, much more complex, context of Broszat's remarks, see his series of letters to Saul Friedlander and Friedlander's excellent replies printed first in *Vierteljahreshefte für Zeitgeschichte* 36, no.2 (April 1988), pp.339-72, subsequently translated and reprinted as 'Martin Broszat/Saul Friedlander: A Controversy about the Historicisation of National Socialism', in *Yad Vashem Studies* 19 (Fall 1988), pp.1-47; also reprinted in *New German Critique* 44 (Spring–Summer 1988), pp.85-126. The exchange between Broszat and Friedlander was initially sparked by Friedlander's response to Broszat's 'Plädoyer für eine Historisierung des Nationalsozialismus' [Plea for a historicisation of National Socialism], *Merkur* 39 (1985), pp.373-85.

   Broszat's specific reference to monuments comes in his comments on 'mythical memory', which he distinguishes from 'scientific insight' (*New German Critique* 44 [Spring–Summer 1988], pp.90-1).

Fig.50 President Jimmy Carter bows his head in front of the Warsaw Ghetto Monument just before beginning his peace talks between Egypt and Israel, 31 December 1977

7. Rosalind Krauss, *The Originality of the Avant-Garde and Other Modernist Myths* (Cambridge, Mass. and London, 1988), p.280.

8. Pierre Nora, 'Between Memory and History: *Les Lieux de Mémoire*', trans. Marc Roudebush, *Representations* 26 (1989), p.13. Reprinted from Pierre Nora, 'Entre Mémoire et Histoire', *Les Lieux de Mémoire*, Vol.1: *La République* (Paris, 1984), p.xxvi.

9. John Hallmark Neff, 'Introduction [to Public Art]: Daring to Dream', *Critical Inquiry* 16 (Summer 1990), p.857.

10. See Maurice Halbwachs, *Les cadres sociaux de la mémoire* (Presses Universitaires de France, Paris, 1952); also see his *La mémoire collective* (Paris, 1950).

11. See the catalogue for this exhibition, edited by Werner Fenz, *Bezugspunkte 38/88* (Steirischer Herbst, Veranstaltungs-gesellschaft m.b.H, Graz, 1988).

12. For insights into this project by both the artist and curator, see Hans Haacke, 'Und ihr habt doch gesiegt, 1988', and Werner Fenz, 'The Monument Is Invisible, the Sign Visible', in *October* 48 (Spring 1989), pp.75-8; pp.79-87.

13. See Albert Elsen, 'What We Have Learned about Modern Public Sculpture: Ten Propositions', *Art Journal* 48, no.4 (Winter 1989), p.291.; also see Albert Elsen, *Rodin's 'Thinker' and the Dilemmas of Modern Public Sculpture*: (Yale University Press, New Haven, 1985).

Without being too facetious in this context, we might speculate on what a monument to the Holocaust by video artist, Nam June Paik, might look like. Would it be a single video loop, replaying over and over images set in a concentration camp or deportation site? Or would he make an all-purpose monument, a chunk of marble, inset with a video monitor that played any memorial loop we wanted to insert? Depending on the day and location, this stone and video might commemorate Auschwitz, Hiroshima or the First World War – not to mention any number of future catastrophes.

14. For elaboration of this theme, see Matthias Winzen, 'The Need for Public Representation and the Burden of the German Past', *Art Journal* 48 (Winter 1989), pp.309-14.

15. For more elaborate discussions of counter-monuments by the Gerzes, Hoheisel and Radermacher, see James E. Young, 'The Counter-monument: Memory against Itself in Germany Today', *Critical Inquiry* 18 (Winter 1992) pp.267-96.

16. Henry Moore, 'The Auschwitz Competition', booklet published by the State Museum of Auschwitz, 1964, unpaginated.

17. For examples, see Albert E. Elsen, *Modern European Sculpture, 1918-1945: Unknown Beings and Other Realities*, (George Braziller, Inc, New York, 1979), pp.122-5.

18. See Janet Blatter, 'Art from the Whirlwind', in Janet Blatter and Sybil Milton, eds *Art of the Holocaust* (Pan Books, London, 1982), pp.22-35.

19. See Peter Bürger, *The Theory of the Avant Garde*, trans. Michael Shaw (University of Minnesota Press, Minneapolis, 1984), p.87. Bürger defines the 'functional analysis of art' as an examination the artwork's 'social effect (function), which is the result of the coming together of stimuli emanating from within the work itself and a sociologically definable public ...'

20. Marianne Doezema, 'The Public Monument in Tradition and Transition', in *The Public Monument and Its Audience* (Cleveland Museum of Art, Cleveland, 1977), p.9.

21. Robert Musil, 'Monuments', in *Posthumous Papers of a Living Author*, trans. Peter Wortsman (Eridanos Press Inc., Hygiene, Colorado, 1987), p.61.

22. I suggested a similar critique of monuments in much rougher form in 'Memory and Monument', in Geoffrey H. Hartman, ed. *Bitburg in Moral and Political Perspective* (Indiana University Press, Bloomington, 1986), p.112; reprinted in expanded form in James E. Young, *Writing and Rewriting the Holocaust: Narrative and the Consequences of Interpretation* (Indiana University Press, Bloomington, 1988).

For an excellent, much more fully adumbrated discussion of 'the struggle between iconoclasm and idolatry', see W. J. T. Mitchell, *Iconology: Image, Text, Ideology* (University of Chicago Press, Chicago and London, 1986), pp.160-208.

23. For a full-fledged enactment of the kind of critique I am proposing here, in which I tell the 'biographies' of dozens of Holocaust memorials located in Germany, Austria, Poland, Israel and America, see my *The Texture of Memory: Holocaust Memorials in History* (Yale University Press, New Haven and London, 1993).

Also see James E. Young, 'The Biography of a Memorial Icon: Nathan Rapoport's Warsaw Ghetto Monument', *Representations* 26 (Spring 1989), pp.69-106.

James E. Young is Professor of English and Judaic Studies at the University of Massachusetts, Amherst and the author of *The Texture of Memory* (1993) and *Writing and Rewriting the Holocaust* (1988). He was also Guest Curator for the exhibition *The Art of Memory: Holocaust Memorials in History* at the Jewish Museum in New York City (1994), which travelled to the Deutsches Historisches Museum in Berlin and the Stadt Museum in Munich, and he was Editor of *The Art of Memory* (1994).

Monica Bohm-Duchen

Fifty Years On

Theodor Adorno's much-quoted maxim – to which the title of this volume and this exhibition implicitly refers – that 'to write a poem after Auschwitz is barbaric', raises profound moral issues that artists in any medium would be foolhardy to ignore. The complex relationship between culture and barbarism, and the dangers inherent in the aestheticisation of horror, are indisputably issues of continuing relevance. We should remember, however, that the words were penned in 1949,[1] when the shock of the camps was all too raw. Yet even then, as other essays in this catalogue show, artists, both survivors and those less directly affected by the Holocaust, felt compelled to grapple with the subject in their art. These days, in a world witnessing a disturbing resurgence of tribal nationalism, neo-Fascism and anti-Semitism, there seems to be an ever-increasing number of visual artists, Jews and non-Jews alike, working with the theme. All this suggests that artists both then and now subscribe less to Adorno's striking but ultimately dismissive claim, than to survivor Elie Wiesel's memorable admission of an irresolvable paradox: 'How is one to speak of it? How is one not to speak of it?'[2] Indeed, an acknowledgement of the complexity, not to say the impossibility of the task in hand lies at the heart of the best and most powerful art created on the subject. That, and a conviction that art's ability, or otherwise, to deal with the most significant event of the twentieth century can be seen as a crucial gauge of art's credentials in post-war society.

For many artists born since the Second World War it is no longer enough to reproduce the images of horror – the barbed wire, the crematoria, the skeletal survivors, the emaciated corpses – in a doomed attempt to re-create a sense of how it was. It may indeed be the case, as many have claimed, that only those who lived through the Holocaust themselves have the right to speak (in whatever medium) on behalf of those who did not survive. Yet, as George Steiner has so forcefully put it, even those of an older generation who did not experience the Holocaust at first-hand have a

right to confront it on their own terms: 'because the black mystery of what happened in Europe is to me indivisible from my own identity. Precisely because I was not there, because an accident of good fortune struck my name from the roll'.[3] A post-war generation has its own concerns and obligations: not just to look backwards in mourning or nostalgia (although the need to mourn persists), but to grapple with the contemporary significance of the Holocaust, 'which is not the event itself, but *memory* of the event, the great distance between then and now, between here and there'.[4] To this day, and in spite of the huge numbers of words and images devoted to the subject, the Holocaust (for which the word 'Auschwitz' stands only as a symbol, justifiably the most notorious part of a far more complex whole) defies complete understanding, yet constantly compels us to try to understand.

Media coverage of the numerous other catastrophes, both natural and man-made, that have occurred since the Second World War has, sadly, inured most of us to the reality of suffering. If a corpse, a distraught mother, an orphaned child caught by the camera fail to move us as they should, the chances of our responding adequately to their realistic depiction in bronze or paint are slimmer still. Even in the immediate post-war period, sincere attempts by artists to re-create 'how it was' paled into insignificance beside the documentary evidence – those terrible photographs taken at the liberation of the camps, which, in Susan Sontag's words, 'gained the status of ethical reference points'. Yet, as Sontag herself admits, even these are 'in danger of losing their emotional charge'. 'At the time of the first photographs of the Nazi camps, there was nothing banal about these images. After thirty [and how much more, after fifty!] years, a saturation point may have been reached. In these last decades, "concerned" photography has done as much to deaden conscience as to arouse it.'[5]

Yet the challenge of those corpses remains. For survivor artists such as Zoran Music, Isaac Celnikier and Ronny Abram, they continue – not surprisingly, for

Cat. numbers refer to the List of Works in Exhibition on p.157

these are men who actually witnessed the grim reality at first-hand – to be little short of an obsession. The problems, however, of communicating the sheer scale of the suffering, and of avoiding any hint of dubious eroticism, persist. The most moving of Music's post-war images are, it seems to me, the most understated, those which merely hint at the vast numbers of victims, depicting a few in detail and hesitantly sketching in the contours of the rest. The generic title of these works, *We Are Not the Last* (see Cats 44-8 and Col.Fig.34), renders their message both universal and contemporary, without, however, detracting from the specificity of the original source material. The undeniable, almost sensual beauty of the handling of paint (or the graphic medium, as the case may be) remains in necessary and poignant tension with the horrific subject-matter. Thinking again of Adorno's famous maxim, might it not be the case that just *because* German culture did not prevent German barbarism, some might conceive it a duty of post-Auschwitz society to nurture culture's redemptive role, to prevent further barbarism? Another survivor featured in this exhibition, Daisy Brand, who, like Music (and so many other Holocaust survivors), repressed her need to confront the past until relatively recently, has spoken of her – possibly utopian, but undoubtedly sincere – belief in the power of art to restore the balance between good and evil, hope and despair. There is little doubt that the making of art directly related to the artist-survivor's wartime experience fulfils a cathartic, and hence positive function for that individual, as Kitty Klaidman, also featured here, has confirmed.

Artists who use the all-too-familiar images of heaped-up corpses at second-hand run further risks. When, for example, the American Protestant artist Robert Morris bases his baroque, apocalyptic compositions (see Col.Fig.28) on the well-known photographs of camp victims already mentioned, the dangers of sensationalising and eroticising the subject-matter, however unintentionally, are hard to avoid. Natan Nuchi, the Israeli-born child of a Holocaust survivor,

seeks to escape this danger, and more generally the stereotypical and predictable, by isolating single figures and setting them against a sombre, abstract and spatially ambiguous backdrop, so that they become iconic and emblematic. The source of these images is unmistakable and specific, their implications universal. The Holocaust victim becomes all victims, Christlike in his suffering,[6] his nakedness the ultimate challenge to the post-Renaissance Western tradition of the heroic male nude (See Col.Fig.54).

Art which relies too faithfully on other aspects of the Holocaust known to most of us only through photographs often runs the risk of seeming clichéd and stereotypical, incapable of provoking a fresh response to the subject. Emaciated figures in striped camp uniform complete with yellow star, brutal Nazi guards, watchtowers, railway tracks, barbed wire – all these, although indisputably a quintessential part of the Holocaust landscape, have become over-used to the point of losing all power to shock. However deeply felt and expressionistically handled (as in the work of survivors David Bloch and Edith Birkin, and 'empathisers' such as Bruce Carter, Andrew Aarons and Marlene Miller), the necessary grotesqueness of the imagery tends only to repel, its predictability and over-explicitness, forming – although one hesitates to say this – a kind of 'Holocaust kitsch'.[7]

Other artists have sought to address the central problem of rendering the de-humanised human body by less historically specific means. The well-meaning attempts of artists of a naturalist or expressionist persuasion (sculptors such as George Anthonissen and Deborah Sperber and painters and graphic artists such as Philip Zuchman, Armando, Selma Waldman, Roger Loewig and Jerome Witkin) to adapt an existing vocabulary of anguished human forms to provide a commentary on the suffering endured in the Holocaust too often lead to imagery that, while frequently powerful, tends to be somewhat predictable, crude and over-explicit.

More successful (because less explicit) are works

Col.Fig.51 George
Segal's *Holocaust*, at
the Legion of Honor in
San Francisco, view
towards the Pacific
Ocean, 1983

Col.Fig.52 One of the
stones in Jochen Gerz's
*2146 Stones: A
Monument Against
Racism*, this one
inscribed to Jugenheim

Col.Fig.53 Detail of graffiti on Harburg's 'Monument against Fascism'

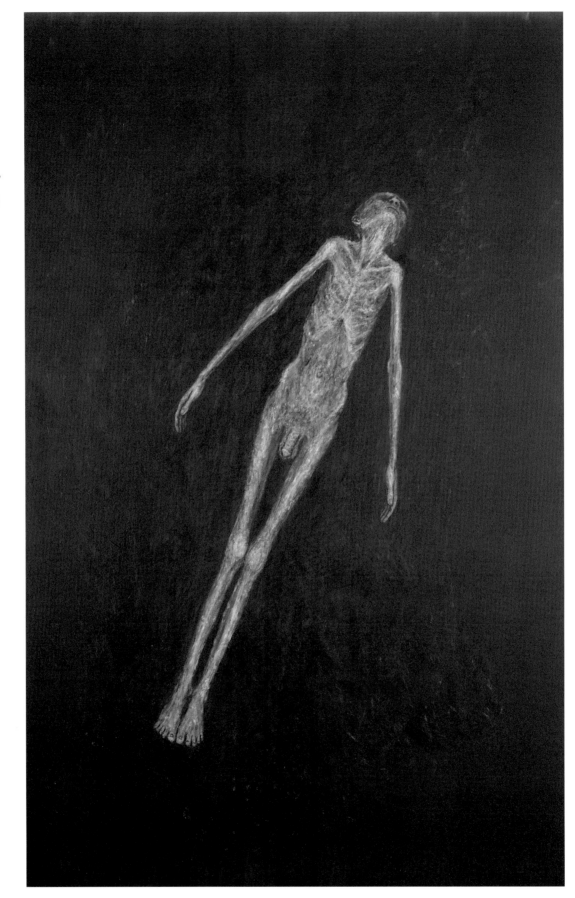

Col.Fig.54 Natan
Nuchi, *Untitled*, 1991,
acrylic on canvas,
2.74 × 1.72 m (Cat.51)

Col.Fig.55 Shimon
Attie, *Mulackstrasse
37: Slide Projection of
Former Jewish Residents
(c.1932)*, from *Writing
on the Wall* series, 1991,
C-type photograph,
50 × 60 cm (Cat.2d)

Col.Fig.56 Magdalena
Abakanowicz, *Backs*,
1976 - 82, burlap and
glue, 80 figures, 3 sizes:
61 × 50 × 55 cm/69 × 56 ×
66 cm/72 × 59 × 69 cm

Fig.57 Magdalena
Abakanowicz, *Cast
Standing Figures '94*, 1994,
bronze, 20 figures, each
*c.*1.85 m × 50 cm × 97 cm

Col.Fig.58 Sally Heywood, *The Reconstruction of the Synagogue*, 1991, oil on canvas, 1.60 × 2 m (Cat.18)

Col.Fig.59 Sally Heywood, *The Burning*, 1993, oil on canvas, 1.90 × 2.50 m (Cat.20)

Col.Fig.60 Daisy Brand, *The Broken Promise* (triptych), 1990, porcelain, earthenware and wood, 84 × 96.5 × 10 cm (Cat.6)

Col.Fig.61 Daisy Brand, *Last Trip*, 1990, porcelain and wood, 84 × 42 × 10 cm (Cat.7)

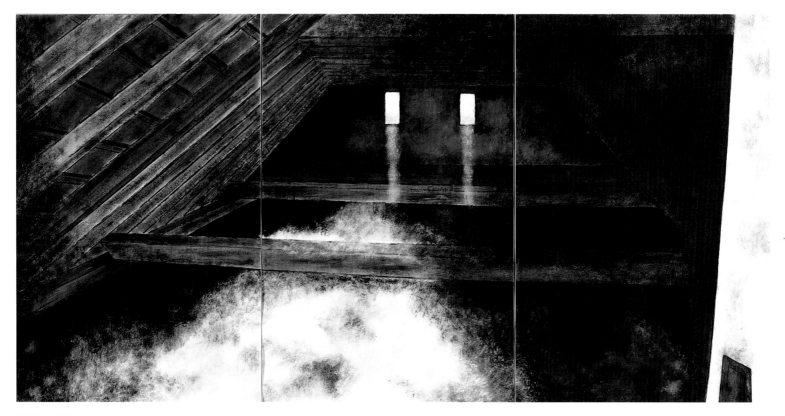

Col.Fig.62 Kitty
Klaidman, *Hidden
Memories: Attic in
Humence* (triptych),
1991, acrylic on paper,
3.05 × 1.52 m (Cat.27)

Col.Fig.63 Kitty Klaidman, *Looking Down II*, 1991, acrylic on paper, 1.52 × 1.02 m

Col.Fig.64 Elyse
Klaidman, *The Attic*,
1992, oil on canvas,
1.07 m × 91 cm

Col.Fig.65 John Goto,
Rembrandt in Terezin,
1983 - 8, oil paint on
photograph,
1.54 × 1.27 m (Cat.17)

Col.Fig.66 Ellen Rothenberg, *The Combing Shawl*, 1993, text of the *Diary of Anne Frank* printed on vellum, graphite, aluminium and steel brackets, 350 combs cast in various metals, 1.83 × 1.07 × 2.44 m (Cat.56)

Col.Fig.67 Fabio Mauri,
*Western or Wailing
Wall*, 1993, leather (real
suitcases), wood,
canvas, 4 m × 4 m
× 80 cm (Cat.43)

Col.Fig.68 Nancy Spero, *The Ballad of Marie Sanders*, hand printing on walls, installation at Jewish Museum, New York, 1993

Col.Fig.70 Deborah Davidson, *Trace*, 1992, book installation: monotype, letraset and xerox transfers on handmade paper, 4.27 × 1.83 m (Cat.16)

Col.Fig.71 Lena Liv, *Memoria di nero e blu* [Memory of Black and Blue], 1991 - 2, iron, macrodevelopment of photographic spectrum, handmade paper, pigment, 1.81 m × 87 cm × 31 cm (Cat.41)

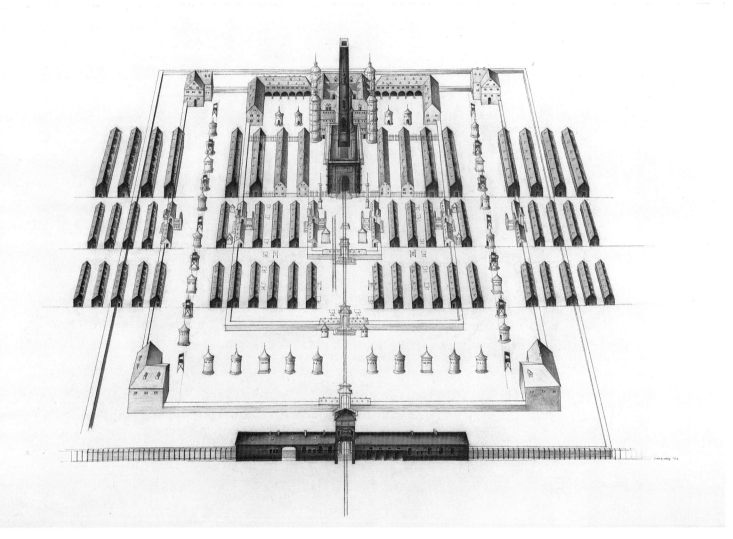

Col.Fig.72 Melvin
Charney, *Visions of the
Temple (after Matthias
Haffenreffer's
'Reconstruction of the
Temple of Jerusalem',
Tübingen, 1631)*, 1986,
pastel on wove paper,
1.01 × 1.54 m (Cat.14)

Col.Fig.73 Mick
Rooney, *Into the Hands
of Strangers*, 1989,
acrylic/oil on paper,
1.30 × 1.02 m (Cat.53)

Fig.74 Shirley
Samberg, figures from
Wrappings series,
1985 - 93, burlap,
various sizes (see
Cat.57)

that are essentially more ambiguous, less susceptible to single readings. The monumental figures created by the Polish-Catholic sculptor Magdalena Abakanowicz, for example, speak powerfully of the dignity of the victim, however physically mutilated his or her body may be, of vulnerability as an essential part of the human condition. Her large groups of figures – each identical, anonymous, faceless – brilliantly evoke the dehumanisation wrought by mass suffering, while the single figures are no less moving for their distillation of emotion (see Col.Fig.56 and Fig.57). Her favoured material, burlap, reflects her view of the body as being 'like a piece of fabric ... [to] be torn apart with ease', a view formed by her childhood experience of Nazi atrocities, and compounded by her later experience of life under communism. (More recently, she has worked in bronze, but achieves a weathered, patinated surface far removed from the heroic associations of burnished metal.)

In her *Wrappings* series of lifesize burlap figures (see Fig.74), Shirley Samberg, like Abakanowicz, uses cloth as much for its psychological as for its aesthetic properties, to evoke in her case a sense of bandaging as a form of protective covering: but what has become of the bodies underneath? Her figures, although indisputably victims, carry within them a strong hint of menace, which serves to undermine the viewer's faith in a clear distinction between victim and perpetrator. (In a quite different mode, the extraordinary series of paintings entitled *Exit* by American artist Anna Bialobroda explores a similar ambiguity of identity. Prompted by the complexity of his relationship with a young German woman, Israeli installation artist Haim Maor is also concerned with investigating these disquieting grey areas.) Whereas Abakanowicz's artistic references are primarily earthy and primitivistic, Samberg's work alludes to a more mainstream Western tradition, to Gothic cathedral sculptures and Rodin's *Burghers of Calais*. Another American artist, Gabrielle Rossmer, deploys groups of shrouded anthropomorphic forms made of plaster-

impregnated cloth to considerable effect; but counters the more universalising thrust of these figures by juxtaposing them with collaged images and documentation based on her own family history.

Certain painters have remained faithful to the human figure in their attempts to grapple with the Holocaust and its implications, but have chosen an essentially symbolic approach. In a recent series of suggestively understated drawings, South American-born, London-resident Glenn Sujo has made use of the centuries-old tradition of the Vanitas still-life (of which the skull is an integral part) to allude to the suffering endured in the Holocaust and to his own perception of the fragility of things as formed by his ever-growing awareness of its legacy. R. B. Kitaj's preoccupation with a 'diasporist' mentality[8] and its expression in art, and with the meaning of Jewishness in a post-Holocaust world is well known, not to say notorious in a British art world not known for its frank assertions of ethnic allegiances. Since the late 1970s Kitaj has sought – following an already well-established tradition – to create a symbol of Jewish suffering in the Holocaust that would be the equivalent of the Christian cross as the symbol of Christ's martyrdom, and has espoused the crematorium chimney as that symbol. The title, as well as the imagery of his 1985 series of paintings, *Passion (1940-5)* (Cats 21-5) confirms this search for a christological parallel. Unlike so much Holocaust-related art, which, perhaps unsurprisingly, favours a muted, sombre palette, the colours that Kitaj deploys are strong and vibrant, sometimes even discordant. In the same way many of his ambitious figure compositions contain deliberate iconographic disjunctions, as if to draw attention to the impossibility of harmony, the unreliability of cultural referents after the total rupture caused by the Holocaust (see Fig.75).

Mick Rooney, a non-Jewish artist whose awareness of the Holocaust dates back to his boyhood exposure to the shocking newsreels released for public consumption in immediate post-war Britain, was prompted to express his artistic response to the subject only many years later, on reading the novels, essays and poems of Primo Levi. (As a survivor, and a writer of consummate lucidity who against all the odds maintained an extraordinary dispassionateness when writing of the past, Levi became for many a figure of almost iconic authority. Other visual artists have paid tribute to him too: consider, for example, Larry Rivers's *Primo Levi, Witness* of 1988 and the work of Renzo Galleoti.) Non-naturalistic in colour and spatially claustrophobic, Rooney's paintings are densely packed with incidents derived only loosely from Levi's writings (they are certainly not intended as simple illustrations of his work), inviting the viewer to supply the tragic narratives that are here only hinted at (see Col.Fig.73). American painter Jerome Witkin has been working on a series of monumental canvases, collectively entitled *War and Liberation*, since the late 1970s. The most memorable and original of these is without doubt his triptych *Death as an Usher, Berlin, 1933* of 1979-81, in which a surreal and enigmatic narrative is enacted from left to right with almost cinematic melodrama. His more recent paintings, on the other hand, have sought to render the brutality of the Nazis' onslaught on the bodies of their victims with an equally brutal realism and attention to detail, to such an extent that the images become utterly unpalatable, and the viewer, repelled, is likely to turn away.

Some figurative artists – the Americans Arnold Trachtman and Sid Chafetz, for example – have adopted a more openly and directly didactic approach to their subject. Arnold Trachtman uses many of the graphic devices associated with pre-war anti-Nazi propagandists such as John Heartfield; but being produced after, rather than before, the event, images such as these seem well-intentioned but ultimately somewhat pointless. The best-known exponent of this kind of explicit didacticism is Judy Chicago, whose massive *Holocaust Project* has recently been touring the United States[9] amid considerable controversy. As with her earlier projects, this is no conventional artwork, but a team enterprise that took some years to gestate. Combining painting and photography, tapestry and stained glass, it seeks (in Chicago's own words) to honour 'the memory of the Holocaust's victims while examining the event in a way which demonstrates how much the Jewish experience can teach us all'. Her intentions are undoubtedly honourable (she does, after all, hail from a family of rabbis); but the result is both intellectually and aesthetically naive, guilty of gross over-simplification in its conflation of disparate global issues. In artistic terms, she seems to take her cue mainly from the great tradition of Mexican mural art; but in treating this most difficult and complicated of subjects, her images remain crude and over-explicit.

In a different and quieter mode, Scottish artist Myer Lacome has created a series of quasi-abstract collages in which he openly and rather too glibly equates the suffering endured in the Holocaust with the suffering caused by the civil war in Yugoslavia. *Thirty Facts*, an installation of 1991 by the young British artist Danusia Chitryn, in which thirty striped jackets are labelled with the names of thirty locations where human rights have been horribly abused, is another example of this well-meaning but rather simplistic approach. The defiant assertion 'Never again', so often trotted out when the Holocaust is mentioned, is undoubtedly an admirable motive for creating art on the subject, but is, alas, no guarantee of powerful and thought-provoking art. Art *does* have power: not, unfortunately, to change the course of history, or even to stop the recurrence of genocide; but to cast new and sometimes unexpected light on a subject by moving the spectator emotionally, spiritually and intellectually, and by prompting discussion and debate.

There *are* more effective ways of making political statements about the Holocaust in art; but these, although focused on the present, tend to be more historically specific. (For all that the Holocaust can teach lessons of universal relevance, it remains a unique historical phenomenon. Those who speak of 'Holocausts' in the plural are usually, although not always, well-

Fig.75 R. B. Kitaj, *Yiddish Hamlet (Y. Löwy)*, 1985, oil on canvas, 1.22 m × 61 cm (Cat.26)

intentioned; but to do so involves a distortion of history and an evasion of certain key issues.[10]) Photography, with its ineluctable testimonial credentials, is often a crucial component of this work, which frequently involves elements of installation and/or performance art as well. American artist Shimon Attie, resident in Berlin during the last few years, has combed the archives there for photographs of pre-war German-Jewish street life and has slide-projected those images, where possible, on to the very geographical locations where those pictures were taken (see Col.Fig.55). Once done (and this itself can be seen as a kind of 'happening' or form of installation art), what remain are haunting colour photographs that people contemporary Berlin with ghosts of its vanished population. Another, more recent project by Attie was to have involved the slide projection of photographic portraits of former Jewish citizens on to the shopping mall at Hamburg Central Train Station – a politically-charged and subversive act to which the city authorities soon put a stop. (He was later able to execute a similar installation in Dresden.) Canadian artist Melvin Charney met with a similar squeamishness on the part of the German authorities when at the 1981 Kassel *Documenta* he proposed to construct a replica of the façade of the notorious gateway of Birkenau death camp in the middle of contemporary Kassel. All that remains of that aborted project is a powerful series of drawings and photomontages, ironically entitled *Better if they think they are going to a farm* ... (see Cat.10).

German photographer Henning Langenheim in his on-going series *Memorials* takes apparently deadpan, 'straight' black-and-white documentary photographs of the sites of destruction, by means of which he cunningly alerts the viewer to the complexities and ironies of the ways in which the Holocaust is remembered (see Figs 76 and 77). Although visually compelling, the images which dwell on the grim physical remains – a bone, a fragment of skull thrown up in an otherwise barren landscape – are tinged with a note of

Fig.76 Henning
Langenheim, *Dachau
1987: Grass*, from
Memorials series,
b/w photograph,
30 × 37.5 cm (Cat.34)

romantic melancholy that some might see as inappropriate to the subject. More incisive and telling are those which highlight the apparent ordinariness of these places today, the way in which the sites of unspeakable atrocities have been rendered anodyne, fit for tourist consumption. (English photographer Robin Dance works in a similar, even more low-key mode.) This unsavoury, yet perhaps inevitable transformation of concentration camps into tourist attractions has concerned other artists too: Monia Yahia, for example, has gone so far as to create a fold-out series of colour picture postcards of the death camps entitled *KZ* [*Konzentrationslager* or Concentration Camp] *Tours* – a brazen act of irony that, sadly, rings all too true.

Although the names of many camps (Auschwitz, Dachau, Buchenwald and others) have become almost household words, there are some – smaller, more remote – that are only today coming to light. The most recent photographs in Langenheim's *Memorials* series were taken in Belarus and Latvia: one of the most striking and ironic of these depicts the site of a former extermination camp, Maly Trostenets, which now serves as a dumping-ground for discredited Soviet memorials (see Cat.38). English artist Pam Skelton, in her recent video installation piece *Dangerous Places – Ponar*, juxtaposes filmed images of the site of a little-known execution site in Lithuania as it appears today – empty and apparently innocuous – with the recorded voice of one of its few survivors recalling, as he revisits it, the terrible ordeals suffered there. Interspersed with the images of the camp is fragmentary footage of life among the ruins in present-day Vilnius. Little further commentary is needed.

Since the early 1980s, Rumanian-born, Canadian-resident artist Peter Krausz has concerned himself with similar issues, producing painterly meditations on the nature of evil and suffering as evidenced in the sites of cataclysmic political and human events – sites that serve (in his own words) as repositories 'for the personal and collective, conscious and subconscious, memory'. (The evil perpetrated by the Soviet regime in Siberia exercises him almost as much as do the crimes of the Nazis.) Many of his mixed-media works are monumental in scale, ambitious in intention and prone to a certain grandiloquence. More eloquent than these is a series of small-scale paintings on copper he produced in the late 1980s: entitled *Night Train*, this is a sequence of sketchily rendered, ordinary-seeming landscapes inspired by the Claude Lanzmann film *Shoah*[11] – 'the documentary about the Holocaust and the banality of evil. I would like the paintings to be seen as from the windows of a train moving through a banal, sometimes pretty landscape. But to what destination?' Another work, *De Natura (Humana)* of 1992, is similarly devastating in its simplicity, comprising a series of deliberately out-of-focus, unnaturally green colour photographs of a naked man in a public shower. What could be more ordinary? Except that once we absorb what showers signified in the Holocaust, even a shower can never be ordinary again. (The same can hold true for other aspects of the everyday environment, be it chimneys or trains, as Lily R. Markiewicz has intimated in some of her video pieces.)

The young British painter Sally Heywood, on a residency in Berlin in 1990 (just after the Wall came down), was, she tells us, so struck by a domed building close to where she was living that she started painting it – well before she realised its historical and emotional significance. When she discovered that the building in question (ruined but in the process of being restored) had been the main synagogue in that part of the city, 'I had to look no further for my work in Berlin'. The personal recollections of the older people, both Jewish and non-Jewish, who accosted her as she was drawing on the street, her strong awareness of German neo-Nazism and Germans' reluctance to face their own past, an almost visionary experience of seeing a red glow emanate from the building on a cold winter's night (evocative, as she later realised, of the burning of synagogues on Kristallnacht in 1938) – all this compounded her perception of the site, so that the synagogue became for her a symbol of Berlin today. The result in visual terms is a series of strongly coloured, abstracted and painterly images stylistically reminiscent of the work of David Bomberg and Frank Auerbach, but more intense and apocalyptic in their implications (see Col. Figs 58 and 59).

The role of landscape and architecture as innocent or complicitous witnesses to the horror of the Holocaust has proved a fruitful line of enquiry for many other artists too. The best known of these is probably Anselm Kiefer, whose explorations of the legacy of Nazism from a German point of view have proved both compelling and controversial. Most directly focused on the Holocaust is the series of monumental mixed-media canvases he produced in the early 1980s, entitled either *Margarete* or *Shulamith*. The titles pay homage to the extraordinary poem *Todesfuge* or *Death Fugue* written by survivor Paul Celan in a concentration camp in 1945 (and published in 1952), which is rhythmically punctuated with references to 'your golden hair Margarete ... your ashen hair Shulamith', and ends with the following lines:

> a man lives in the house your golden hair Margarete
> he sets his pack on to us he grants us a grave in the air
> he plays with the serpents and daydreams death is
>   master from Germany
>
> your golden hair Margarete
> your ashen hair Shulamith

The Aryan maiden Margarete's golden hair metamorphoses into straw, with its ironically idyllic landscape references; while the dark hair of the Semitic Shulamith is turned ashen by the crematoria ovens. Significantly, the power of each archetype is dependent on the existence – real or implied – of the other: painted images of Shulamith frequently have straw added to them; while a painted black line or curve may echo the shape of Margarete's abstracted straw locks. In one monumental canvas, *Shulamith* of 1983, tribute is paid to the suffering of the Jews by replacing the torches in the Funeral Hall for the Great

German Soldiers (designed by Kreis in *c.*1939) with a seven-flamed Jewish memorial candelabrum. Just as the two women are inseparable in Celan's poem, so Kiefer believes that by destroying its Jewish population, Germany destroyed part of itself; and in symbolically reuniting the two in his own work, attempts to right a terrible wrong. He returned to these themes in the early 1990s with a series of book works entitled *Shulamith*, in which real hair poignantly and shockingly alludes to the Jewish victim.

Many view Kiefer's preoccupation, not to say his fascination with the Nazi past, as deeply and necessarily suspect. It is certainly true that his paintings do not readily reveal their meanings, that ultimately they retain a disturbing ambiguity. It is, I would argue, precisely this underlying tension that makes his work so interesting. The glamour and allure of Nazism has exercised a number of other artists too – Jewish ones included. David Levinthal's deliberately soft-focus colour photographs of models of Nazi leaders involved in rabble-rousing ceremonies are disquieting in the extreme, while Maciej Toporowicz's manipulated photographs (displayed in 1994 on the streets of New York) take a thought-provoking and critical look at the way the idealised image of the nude so beloved of Nazism has survived into our own time in countless advertisements – those for Calvin Klein in particular.

Melvin Charney has addressed himself to an area of cultural enquiry that, regarded almost as a taboo subject, has gone unanalysed for far too long: namely, the death camps as extreme examples of modern architectural thinking. In particular, he has explored the disconcerting similarities he noticed between the architectural layout of the camps and images of the Temple of Jerusalem as depicted by seventeenth- and eighteenth-century French and German visionaries (see Col.Fig.55). The implications of these similarities are disturbing in the extreme, raising important questions about the relationship between architecture and humanism, politics and religion, idealism and terror. Other drawings by Charney, of a more dramatic, even

Fig.77 Henning
Langenheim, *Sobibor
1987: Mass Grave*, from
Memorials series,
b/w photograph,
41 × 33.5 cm (Cat.31)

apocalyptic nature, evoke a nightmare world, predominantly and symbolically red in hue, in which railway lines and chimneys, Piranesi-like, dominate the cityscape, and lurk behind Renaissance façades.

The small-scale ceramic sculptures of Daisy Brand are also obsessed with architectural forms (see Col.Figs 60 and 61). In her case, however, the obsession is deeply and directly rooted in first-hand experience: as a young teenager, she survived no fewer than seven camps in one year, including Auschwitz. Significantly, the empty corridors, the gates, the railway tracks that recur as leitmotifs in her work speak more eloquently in their unpeopled state of the suffering that took place there, and of the strength of her memories, than the occasional, slightly stereotypical figure of a guard or hunched waiting figure. These recurrent architectural elements combine with elegantly stylised, symbolic motifs, such as scrolls and banners abstracted from the striped uniforms of the camp inmates, to create exquisitely crafted, suggestively textured works which are heartbreaking in their restraint, their ability – against all the odds – to create beauty out of hell.

Kitty Klaidman's preoccupation with architectural forms also has an autobiographical basis. As a child in Czechoslovakia, she spent a year of the war in hiding with her family in the storeroom of a gentile farmhouse. Returning there only recently, she has produced a haunting series of paintings inspired by her complex memories of that time. Many of the images allude not to the cramped space in which she was confined, but to the attic space above their heads, reached, on special, rare occasions, by a stepladder, an embodiment of hope and the promise of freedom (see Col.Figs 62 and 63). Ghostly white wraiths, abstract yet anthropomorphic, infuse and illumine the sombre spaces. As with Daisy Brand, abstracted architectural forms stand as metaphors for extreme human experiences and evoke them more powerfully than any figures could. Klaidman has in fact produced a smaller-scale series of photographic collages of a more explicitly figurative nature, in which she pays homage both to her own childhood and, above all, to the people who made it possible for her family to survive. Although more intimate and extremely poignant, these works lack the originality and the suggestiveness of the purely architectural images.

Klaidman's daughter Elyse is also a painter. Interestingly, it was her own experience of visiting Czechoslovakia in her mother's company in the late 1980s that turned her artistic attention to the latter's wartime experiences. While Kitty was painting the woods that surrounded the farmhouse and which had such intense personal significance for her, Elyse Klaidman – of necessity at one remove from the experience – painted portraits, based on old photographs, of family members she never knew. Both women, haunted in different but related ways by the same architectonic elements, then felt compelled to depict the Czech farmhouse that had given the mother shelter. More vividly coloured and emphatic in their handling of paint (she favours oil, Kitty acrylic), the daughter's paintings are paradoxically both more emotional and more detached from their subject than her mother's renderings of similar motifs (see Col.Fig.64).

As father and son, artists Roman and Ardyn Halter offer another fascinating case history. Roman Halter is a survivor, whose paintings and stained glass images derive from a deeply felt humanitarian impulse to convey the horror and the pity of his own wartime experience, and that of so many others who were never able to tell the tale. Like many artists of an older generation, he dwells particularly on the suffering of women and children in order to highlight the tragic pathos of his subject. Sentimentality, however, is averted by a strong graphic awareness. Ardyn Halter is primarily a landscape painter, but in 1981 felt compelled to tackle the subject of the Holocaust in his own way. The result was a series of large-format canvases (now in the permanent collection of the Lohamei Haghetaot Museum in Israel) which combine painted representations of pre-war family photographs with jagged, gothic German script comprising Nazi euphemisms about the annihilation of the Jews, often superimposed on the images like a prison grille. As with Elyse Klaidman, one senses a (no doubt pyschologically necessary) distancing from the trauma of the parent's experience.

Photographers Naomi Salomon and Judah Ein-Mor, in their apparently matter-of-fact representation of artefacts displayed in museums devoted to the Holocaust, provide an effective commentary on the way such objects are both unbearably vivid and impossibly distant. Anyone who has visited Auschwitz or Majdanek, or even the new US Holocaust Memorial Museum in Washington DC will testify to the extraordinary impact made by the huge piles of objects – suitcases, shoes, combs, spectacles, even hair – that once belonged to the victims and are now on display there. Not surprisingly, many artists have worked with this most eloquent of visual evidence, although the relics themselves possess such power that the artist may be hard pressed to produce anything more memorable. Survivor Elsa Pollak, for example, in her monumental clay sculpture *All that Remained* (1985-9, Yad Vashem Art Museum, Jerusalem), replicates in this most fragile of materials a mound of victims' shoes. A number of Lena Liv's complex and allusive mixed-media constructions also incorporate a poignant – although, in her case, barely conscious – reference to these same shoes. Piles of discarded clothes are similarly resonant, as the work of Christian Boltanski, Lily R. Markiewicz and even Stuart Brisley (whose work is *not* specifically concerned with the Holocaust) testifies.

The worn leather suitcases left behind by the victims have caught artists' imaginations in a similar fashion. Since the late 1970s German artist Raffael Rheinsberg has created installations comprising huge piles of real suitcases, both in a gallery and more subversively, in a 'non-art' setting – for example, in front of the Frauenkirche in Munich. In some of his pieces,

the suitcases are left open to reveal their contents: in most cases, an assortment of humble household objects, in others, large numbers of the same items (clothes hangers, rags, corks), immediately suggestive of displacement, dislocation and annihilation. In his monumental *Western or Wailing Wall* of 1993 (Col.Fig.67), Fabio Mauri manages in a brilliant leap of visual imagination to create a wall of these suitcases (disconcertingly Mondrian-like in their geometric configuration), which alludes not only to the Western or Wailing Wall in Jerusalem but to other walls (the Berlin Wall comes immediately to mind) and to other refugees and other victims. An even more recent work comprises a smart, if old-fashioned leather suitcase inscribed in gothic script *'dieser Koffer is arisch'* ['this suitcase is Aryan'] – another arresting gesture that tells the story of discrimination and persecution from a different, but equally illuminating angle (Cat.43a). Of aristocratic Italian parentage, Mauri was deeply traumatised during adolescence by the mysterious disappearance of his Jewish neighbours, but later succeeded in channelling that trauma into a relentless exploration of the meaning of Fascism and anti-Semitism, both past and present, in the form of conceptually-based installation and performance work.

An essentially conceptual approach also characterises the work of Dutch artist Henk Heideveld who in 1990 on Yom HaShoah (Holocaust Remembrance Day) took it upon himself to trace a white line along a railway track from west to east, the direction so many Dutch Jews were forced to travel. According to the artist, he was prevented from completing the 24-kilometre trail he had envisaged by the police, who literally stopped him in his tracks at 12.15 pm. German artist Gunther Demnig made a similarly propitiatory gesture when between 1990 and 1993 he executed his *Spurenlegen* (Leaving Traces) project, in the course of which he inserted commemorative stones into the pavements of Cologne. In 1994 he embarked on his *Stolperstein* (Stumbling Stone) project, which involves inscribing the birth – and when known, death – dates of German Jews deported by the Nazis, and the names of the camps to which they were sent, on concrete plaques, which will then be installed in the form of paving-stones at the addresses where those people once lived. Jochen Gerz's 1993 project *2146 Stones: A Monument against Racism* in Saarbrücken was in part similarly motivated, with the important difference that since in his case no physical trace was left of the politically provocative and emotionally charged act, disturbing questions were deliberately raised about the whole memorialisation process. Other so-called 'anti-monuments', by Gerz and his wife Esther Shalev-Gerz, Horst Hoheisel and Hans Haacke, most of them (perhaps not surprisingly) in Germany, also belong more to the realm of conceptual art than to that of traditional memorial sculpture.[12]

Renata Stih and Frieder Schnock have together produced seemingly innocent images to be posted in public places. Only when one reads the accompanying text (in German) does one realise, with a shock, the political, historical and human implications of their work. A schematised rendering of an academic mortarboard, for example, is accompanied by the words: 'No promotion for Jews 15.4.1937'; while a pretty little cat accompanied by the text 'Jews are no longer allowed to keep pets 15.5.1942' reminds us of another of the Nazi edicts, some more devastating than others, which collectively and progressively served to strip German Jews of their livelihood, their dignity – and ultimately, their lives.

Whether projects such as these can in fact be subsumed under the name of art remains a moot point. Although there is a danger that a primarily conceptual approach can lead to too much detachment and too little emotion, at its best it produces work that is both cerebral and from the heart. In her installation and video pieces, Lily R. Markiewicz, the child of Holocaust survivors, has evolved an understated but powerful symbolic vocabulary to explore the complex issue of post-Holocaust Jewish female identity. Although herself a secularised Jew with a sophisti-

cated grasp of feminist and linguistic theory, her work contains numerous allusions to traditional Jewish ritual practices. In the defiantly titled installation *I Don't Celebrate Christmas* of 1990 (Col.Fig.69), for example, the shrouded mirrors allude on one level (as confirmed by an explanatory text reflected in a mirror above the viewer's head from an unseen source) to the orthodox Jewish practice of covering a mirror with cloth after a death; on another (as confirmed by the photograph of the artist in the act of unveiling – or is it veiling? – a blackened mirror) to the mirror as traditional Western symbol of female vanity. A second photographic panel depicts the darkened, blurred yet reflective surface of a pool of water, adding yet further tantalising ambiguities. The neat piles of folded cloth on the floor likewise contain multiple references: not only to the on-going need to mourn (the use of cloth to cover mirrors is here compounded by a troubling awareness of the piles of clothes left behind by Holocaust victims) and to other traditional Jewish ritual practices such as covering the bread on the Sabbath, but also to female domesticity.

Any sense of detachment in the presentation of these complex ideas is dramatically countered by the mirror that confronts the viewer at the entrance to the installation and brands him or her with the name 'Jew' inscribed at chest-level on its surface, thus colouring one's entire perception of the piece. Other works by Markiewicz employ similar shock tactics: in the tape/slide piece *Silence Woke Me Up Today* (1989), for example, the text is for the most part oblique and allusive, so that the word 'Jew', when it is uttered, comes as a rude shock. Much the same is true of one of Markiewicz's most recent works, *Places to Remember II*, based on her earlier book of almost the same title. In this piece, suggestively abstracted and fragmented photographic images of sand flowing through hands and into a bowl are accompanied by a cyclical, ambient voice recording, which for the most part deals in poetic and non-specific terms with issues of dislocation and alienation; but by the unexpected and abrupt

Fig.78 Christian Boltanski, *Altar to the Chajes High School*, 1987, 4 b/w photographs in metal frames, 88 tin boxes, 4 lamps, 2.23 × 2.38 m (Cat.3)

inclusion of the word 'Jew' roots the haunting general-ities in a highly specific context – that of the 'second generation' attempting to come to terms with the legacy of the Holocaust.

American installation and performance artist Ellen Rothenberg's works also tease the intellect from a specifically female point of view. Since 1990 she has given artistic expression to a long-standing preoccupa-tion with the real-life figure of Anne Frank (the young Jewish-Dutch girl who in hiding wrote a diary which – unlike its author – survived the war) in the form of her *Anne Frank Project*, a tripartite installation con-sisting of *A Partial Index* (1991), *A Probability Bordering on Certainty* (1993) and *The Conditions for Growth* (1994). Her realisation, after reading the criti-cal and unexpurgated version of the *Diary* (published in English in 1989), that earlier editions had elimi-nated nearly all references to the young girl's burgeon-ing sexuality and her troubled relationship with her mother, as well as to the family's German origins and the fact that now, in Amsterdam, they were in hiding from the Germans, prompted Rothenberg to explore the complex ways in which Anne Frank has been mythologised, turned into a kind of Jewish saint stripped of both cultural specificity and individual complexity. In technically inventive and thought-provoking ways, Rothenberg's work invites us to reassess the situation.

A Probability Bordering on Certainty, for example, includes an old-fashioned vitrine, displaying several neat piles of visiting cards, each printed with the words 'Anne Frank, author' in different typefaces – an ingenious reminder of the ways in which identity can be manipulated and constructed. Another vitrine con-tains a pile of pink erasers, each one with the word 'guilt' inscribed on it in gothic letters – a striking ges-ture that smacks perhaps too much of a conceptual joke (the piece is actually titled *Guilt Erasers!*), but nevertheless gives pause for thought. *The Combing Shawl* (Col.Fig.66), which forms part of the same installation, is aesthetically the most resolved of its

component parts: the combing shawl of the title refers to the cape used by Anne when combing her hair; the strands of text (excerpts from the *Diary*) cascade to the floor like women's hair, and the floor is strewn with metal combs, alluding not only to the combing shawl but also (as discussed above) to the huge piles of combs and other artefacts once owned by victims of the Holocaust and now displayed in museums.

By the obvious yet ingenious act of inscribing ordi-nary pencils with Anne Frank's name, another young American artist, Melissa Gould, has explored the troub-ling implications of Anne Frank's elevation to the sta-tus of an icon – and a tourist attraction. Gould, like Rothenberg, is technically inventive and conceptually nimble in her explorations of certain aspects of the Holocaust. A real scrubbing brush, for example, is inscribed with the words 'Souvenir Wien 1938', and two toothbrushes are inscribed with the names Israel and Sara: a darkly ironic reference to an incident in that year when the SS compelled Austrian Jews to scrub the streets of Vienna with their own tooth-brushes. (Sara and Israel were the middle names forced upon Jews in the Nazi period.) Another piece of 1993 by Gould, called *Schadenfreude* (literally, the joy one experiences at another's misfortunes), utilises images from a 1935 German encyclopaedia to create what the artist, with characteristically black humour, calls a 'Nazi Wallpaper Store'. Innocuous at first glance, a closer examination of these images reveals a deeply ironic and tragic dimension. Schematic render-ings of lampshades and soap, for instance, look inno-cent until one remembers that the Nazis actually used human remains in the making of these objects; as does the image of two boys somersaulting, except that together their bodies form the shape of a swastika. Combined with the repeated image of hands sewing on an armband, these serve as a sobering reminder of the appeal of Nazism to young people and the strength of the Hitler Youth.

If aspects of the work of Markiewicz, Rothenberg and Gould reveal a preoccupation with gender-linked

Fig.79 Susanna
Pieratzki, *Birth*, from
Parents series, 1991, 14
b/w photographs, each
26.5 × 26.5 cm (Cat.52f)

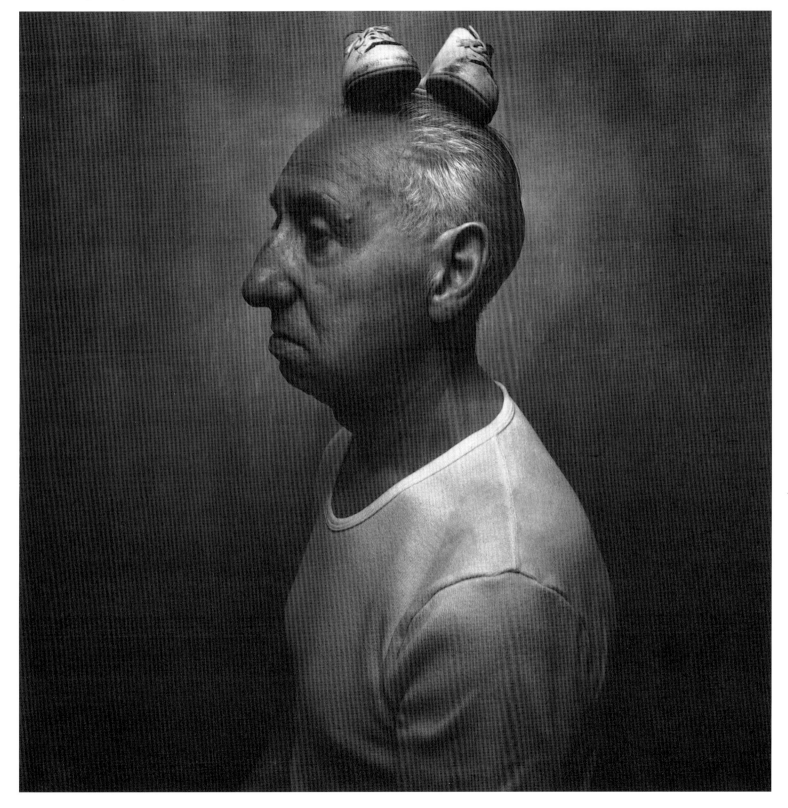

issues, in Nancy Spero's work a feminist preoccupation is absolutely central. Spero has long been known for her wall-pieces, which use text and photographically based images to expose the suffering of women throughout history and in every culture, portraying them both as victims and heroines. Recently, she has turned her attention to the brutalities perpetrated by the Nazis on women who were themselves Jewish or consorted with Jews. *Masha Bruskina* (1993) pays homage to a young Jewish partisan hung by the Nazis, without them realising that she was in fact a Jew; while *The Ballad of Marie Sanders*, of 1993 (Col.Fig.68), pays tribute to the courage of a young Aryan woman who was killed for sleeping with a Jew.

One of the relatively few other artists to concern themselves primarily with the suffering of women in the Nazi era is Yocheved Weinfeld. Born in Poland in 1947, the child of survivors, she spent her first ten years in Poland, haunted by her European past, before her family emigrated to Israel. Since the 1970s much of Weinfeld's work has taken the form of a series of powerful and disquieting mixed-media images, in which she projects herself into the past, casting herself into the role of Holocaust victim. Although both Spero and Weinfeld undoubtedly feel strongly about their subject-matter, the latter's work possesses an urgency and intensity far removed from the more cerebral and indirect approach adopted by Spero.

Photographs of children now grown-up or dead can act as powerful reminders of mortality in any circumstances. If we know that they show children who almost certainly perished in the Holocaust, their poignancy becomes hard to bear. The two works entitled *Altar to the Chajes High School* (Fig.78) and *The Festival of Purim*, which form part of a series called *Lessons of Darkness* produced by French artist Christian Boltanski in the late 1980s, knowingly tread a fine line between sentiment and sentimentality. In both works, over-enlarged and deliberately blurred photographs of Jewish schoolchildren taken just prior to the outbreak of the Second World War are incorpo-

rated into structures reminiscent of a Catholic altar (Boltanski himself is half-Jewish, half-Catholic) – albeit of an unorthodox kind, made up of tin boxes and electric light bulbs! Although some doubt has since been thrown on the authenticity of Boltanski's photographic source material, the poignancy and power of the work persist.

Russian-born, Italian-resident aritst Lena Liv also incorporates images of children into her work. In her case, the photographs hark back to an earlier, inter-war period, and rely for their power on a more generalised sense of the loss of childhood as a metaphor for other forms of loss, including the loss of life in the Holocaust (see Col.Fig.71). More lyrical and carefully crafted than Boltanski's constructions, Liv's mixed-media pieces also rely more on poetic allusiveness. A decorated ball (fashioned, like all the objects in her work, out of hand-made paper pulp) is one of several recurring leitmotifs – held by the child in *Memoria di Arianna*, for example, solemnly, hieratically, like a holy grail (see Cat.39). A toy horse fulfils a similar function, acquiring, like the ball, the status almost of a talisman – one, however, that lacks the power to work the ultimate magic, to halt life, and death, in their tracks.

Susanna Pieratzki is a young German-Jewish photographer whose work focuses not on children as such, but on parents, and her own position as the child of two Holocaust survivors. The series of posed black-and-white photographs she took in 1991, entitled *Parents* (Cat.52), is perhaps the most intimate and personal of all the work included in the current exhibition – which, if we compare it with the far more cerebral work of another second generation artist, Lily R. Markiewicz, goes to prove that it is as difficult to generalise about the art produced by the children of survivors as it is about anything else. In this series, Pieratzki has depicted both her parents in a sequence of symbolically significant poses and accompanied by symbolically significant props, and has given each image a title and a number that speaks of an elemen-

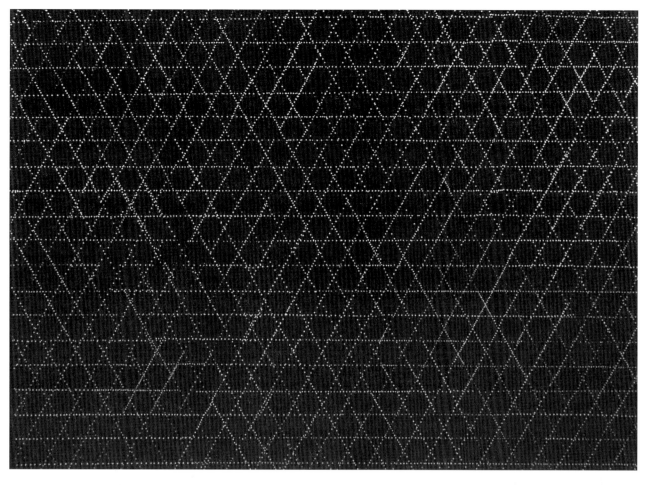

Fig.80 Amanda Guest, *Untitled*, 1993, pinpricks in paper (backlit), 76 × 56 cm

tal life-cycle. *Birth*, for example (Fig.79), shows her father in profile like a Renaissance duke, sad but noble in his suffering, two small shoes resting on his head. The image is an arresting one in visual terms alone; but once we know that the shoes allude to the birth of his daughter Susanna (they reappear in an openly elegiac image called *Remembrance*, the last in the series) it becomes almost unspeakably moving. The same is true of *War*, which depicts her father in striped pyjamas (ordinary enough, but the association with a camp inmate's uniform is hard to avoid) facing away from the camera, eight wire hangers dangling behind his back (the number of hangers is a reference to the eight siblings Pieratzki's father lost in the Holocaust). On another level, the images speak eloquently of two human beings who have survived the Holocaust and managed to retain a great inner strength and beauty, in spite of, perhaps because of, their great inner sadness; and of the daughter's immense respect and tenderness for the parents she can perhaps never fully understand.

John Goto, like so many of the artists discussed in this essay, employs photography and text to further his own exploration of the significance of the Holocaust. Non-Jewish, although of Eastern European descent, he visited the so-called model ghetto of Theresienstadt or Terezin near Prague in 1983, taking a series of 'straight' black-and-white documentary photographs that were later to serve as a kind of prelude to the series of mixed-media images entitled *Terezin* which he produced in the late 1980s (see Col.Fig.65). Terezin was remarkable on a number of counts: most relevant here is the fact that a disproportionate number of those held prisoner there were artists and intellectuals. Actively encouraged by the Nazis, who held Terezin up as proof to the world that the Jews were hardly suffering at all, the inmates created a lively cultural life within its walls – until, that is, most of them were deported to the death camps.

Goto has chosen to focus in particular on the extraordinary figure of Friedl Dicker-Brandeis, an artist trained at the Bauhaus who acted as art teacher to the children of Terezin. References also to Kafka and Rembrandt and artists such as Karel Fleischmann and Bedrich Fritta, who actually worked in Terezin, combine with excerpts from contemporary and post-war texts about Terezin to give expression to Goto's primary preoccupations: namely, an investigation of the way our knowledge of the past is constructed, and above all, of the deeply complex relationship between culture and barbarism. The latter, unsurprisingly, is an issue that exercises many other artists: Pam Skelton's 1993 series of paintings *Dangerous Places – Goethe's Oak*, for example, explores the unresolvable paradox that Buchenwald embraced the site of the poet Goethe's favourite tree. In his 1993 installation *Phoenix*, French artist Jean-Sylvain Bieth reconstructed a library ironically comprising books both banned and 'recommended' by the authorities in occupied France – all of them interspersed with jars containing mysterious and sinister-looking substances. Heinrich Heine's famously prophetic observation that where 'books are burned, people burn also' is never far away.

American artist Susan Erony has confronted the implications of Heine's dictum head-on in a series of mixed-media images, *Memorial to the Jews of Lodz*, which actually incorporates fragments of burnt Hebrew texts which she found discarded in the ruins of the one remaining synagogue in the Polish town of Lodz. American book artist Deborah Davidson uses fragments of text embedded in hand-made paper to pay tribute both to the suffering of her own mother's family in Italy and to the fate of the Italian and Sephardi Jews in general (see Col.Fig.70). Her work is poetic and allusive, elegaic in mood but never sentimental.

Some artists, wary both of over-conceptualising and over-sensationalising the horror of the Holocaust, have avoided figurative references altogether in favour of total abstraction. It is a striking fact that the only contemporary artworks to feature in the US Holocaust Memorial Museum in Washington DC are completely abstract canvases or sculptures by well-known artists such as Sol LeWitt, Richard Serra and Elsworth Kelly. While the actual works differ very little from the artists' usual productions (and could thus be seen as not having any real relevance to the Holocaust), it is surprising how appropriate *in situ* these abstract images seem. Perhaps, in the face of the overwhelming visual documentary evidence contained in the museum, any other kind of art would seem impertinent.[13]

The Israeli artist Moshe Kupferman, himself a survivor, has evolved a restricted but eloquent repertoire of abstract grid forms that work on many levels simultaneously. Although in no way simply illustrative of his wartime experiences, the forms in his paintings do nevertheless evoke a sense of enclosure and incarceration countered by a certain lyricism in the muted colour harmonies. Unequipped with any biographical information about the artist, however, the viewer would be forgiven for missing such references. Survivor Nettie Schwarz Vanderpol has recently turned to the unusual medium of embroidery to express her own coming to terms with the past. Many of her images are completely abstract; but unlike Kupferman, she supplies a verbal commentary that makes the link with the Holocaust quite explicit – a fact which makes the images easier to understand, but ultimately weakens their symbolic and imaginative power. American artist Mindy Weisel is deeply aware of being the child of survivors; yet when faced with her colourful, quasi-abstract paintings, the references to the Holocaust are often so oblique as to be almost invisible. Lee Waisler has evolved a rather too elegant vocabulary of abstract forms to allude symbolically to the Holocaust: once again, however, recourse to a vocabulary which is too arcane renders the work inadequate to the task of communication, and formalism triumphs.

Amanda Guest's small-scale paper works make eloquent and poignant use of the abstract yet symbolically rich form of the Star of David. One work, for example, consists of a yellow cut-out star pierced with thread and wire (a reference, surely, to the infamous

Yellow Star that Jews were forced to sew on to their clothes); another creates a seemingly abstract pattern through the repetition of the star form created by tiny pin-pricks in the paper (Fig.80). Annette Lemieux, an essentially conceptual artist, occasionally works in an apparently abstract mode. In *Points of Departure* (1990), for example, a grid of dots deployed across the picture surface turns out to have been created with cigarette butts; in *Devouring Element* (1990-1), the space between the densely interlocking burn marks creates a pattern of swastikas. The latter is the more historically specific in its references; yet the former work is probably the stronger, just because it is more open-ended.

How, then, is one to create an artwork that is both unequivocally about the Nazi Holocaust yet of relevance today, that is neither too narrow nor too wide in its references, neither too obvious nor too oblique? There are no answers – only a compulsion to go on trying. To quote Wiesel again: 'It has all been said, yet all remains to be said.'[14]

Notes

1. T. W. Adorno, 'Kulturkritik und Gesellschaft', article of 1949, published in 1951, republished in *Prismen: Kulturkritik und Gesellschaft* (1955, 1963, 1969). English translation *Prisms: Cultural Criticism and Society* by S. & S. Weber, (Neville Spearman, London, 1967; MIT Press, Cambridge, Mass, 1981).

2. Elie Wiesel, title essay in *One Generation After*, (Weidenfeld & Nicolson, London, 1971, originally published in French in 1965).

3. George Steiner, 'A Kind of Survivor – for Elie Wiesel', in *Language and Silence*, (Faber & Faber, London, 1979).

4. James E. Young, *The Texture of Memory: Holocaust Memorials and Meaning*, (Yale University Press, New Haven and London, 1993).

5. Susan Sontag, *On Photography*, (Farrar, Straus & Giroux, New York, 1977).

6. The frequent tendency of artists and other cultural commentators to link the Holocaust victim with Christ has already been noted by Ziva Amishai-Maisels, *Depiction and Interpretation: The Influence of the Holocaust on the Visual Arts*, (Routledge, New York, 1981).

7. For a thought-provoking analysis of this phenomenon (though mainly in other media, and with the emphasis on the widespread fascination with Nazism itself), see Saul Friedlander, *Reflections of Nazism: An Essay on Kitsch and Death*, (Indiana University Press, Bloomington and Indianapolis, 1984).

8. See R. B. Kitaj, *First Diasporist Manifesto*, (Thames & Hudson, London, 1989).

9. It has also been published in book form: see Judy Chicago, *The Holocaust Project*, (Viking Penguin, New York, 1993).

10. See Ronnie Landau's essay in this catalogue for a more detailed discussion of this point.

11. The contrast between Lanzmann's 1986 film *Shoah* and Steven Spielberg's *Schindler's List* is a telling one. Spielberg, product of Hollywood that he is, has produced an historical epic, complete with hero and plenty of dramatic and tear-jerking incidents, clearly believing that only an imaginary reconstruction of events could evoke a vivid sense of how it was for a wide, ill-informed and probably incredulous public. Lanzmann, on the other hand, is convinced of the inadvisability – not to say the impossibility – of reconstructing the past in this way. His own film contains no documentary footage whatsoever, and relies primarily on the verbal recollections of individuals (perpetrators as well as victims) who lived through that time. Most fine artists, particularly although not exclusively of a younger generation, favour a more cautious and oblique approach than Spielberg, preferring – like Lanzmann – to confront the Holocaust by way of the present.

12. This type of work is discussed in more detail in James Young's essay in the present catalogue.

13. See Ken Johnson, 'Art and Memory', *Art in America*, November 1993 for a thoughtful discussion of the issues raised by the Museum's choice of artworks.

14. Elie Wiesel, 'Readings' in *One Generation After*, op.cit.

Monica Bohm-Duchen (MA Courtauld Institute of Art) is a London-based freelance writer, lecturer and exhibition organiser with a special interest in the issue of Jewish identity in twentieth-century art, and the experience of immigration and persecution. The institutions for which she has worked include the Tate Gallery, the Royal Academy of Arts and the Open University; the publications to which she has contributed include *The Jewish Quarterly, RA Magazine, Art Monthly* and the catalogue of the Ben Uri Art Society Permanent Collection. She co-curated *Art in Exile in Great Britain 1933-1945*, an exhibition held in Berlin and London (at the Camden Arts Centre) in 1985-6, and acted as researcher and assistant selector for *Chagall to Kitaj: Jewish Experience in Twentieth Century Art* (Barbican Art Gallery, London, 1990). Her monograph on Marc Chagall is to be published by Phaidon Press.

Artists' Statements

Magdalena Abakanowicz
Born Poland 1930, of an aristocratic Catholic family which suffered badly at the hands of the Nazis.
Lives and works in Warsaw.

See Rose, Barbara, *Magdalena Abakanowicz*, Harry N. Abrams Inc, New York, 1994.

BANISHED FROM PARADISE
Perhaps at that time in paradise, while eating the forbidden apple, they lost the balance proper to nature – like one loses the sense of smell or eyesight.

And perhaps at the same moment they acquired the instinct of destruction of the surrounding world and of themselves.

Was there a mistake in the unfailing logic of nature or an act of will of an unknown power?

I was nine years old when it began.

One human tribe having recognised itself as superior, it overpowered others and decided to murder them.

As a little girl, I once caught a rabbit. I held it firmly. It breathed, the ribs of its chest moved like mine. Its eyelids fluttered like mine. Besides that, it was different.

This explained why killing it for economic needs was normal.

I looked at the invaders, at their faces. I counted how many fingers their hands had. They walked on two legs. I couldn't find any difference between us and them.

They organised the extermination of millions swiftly and economically. They hunted us down in homes, in streets, in fields. Then packed us tightly into freight trains and sent us to death factories also known as concentration camps.

First they washed people, then shaved them. After being suffocated in gas chambers the bodies were rendered for fat. Then cremated. Ashes were spread on fields to get abundant crops, especially of cabbage.

I remember a woman whispering in the shop: don't buy that soap, someone found a human nail in it.

I remember my mother saying: oh, God, this brush is made out of human hair!

I remember people recounting: they tried to tan human skin but it proved too stretchy.

Where is your brother Abel?

Humans always murdered humans, trying to justify it by ideology, religion, patriotism, philosophy.

It developed in our time into an industrial process carried on by the Nazis.

It became a test of the newest technology in Hiroshima and deprived death of dignity in the Yugoslavia and Rwanda massacres.

I survived.

Grown up, I escaped from reality into art. At the beginning I believed that art is the harmless activity of mankind. But I was witness of its use for propaganda purposes by totalitarian systems.

I believed in the extraordinary sensitivity of an artist, but I learned that Hitler was a painter and Stalin used to write sonnets.

Running away from political pressure into my dreams, I found myself caught by longings, disappointments and fears similar to those that have accompanied human existence from its very beginning.

I bewitch my time filling it with forms, crowds of figures and objects.

As though building a barrier, a fence, a wall that could protect me.

Behind it I feel safe. I can speak to people through the metaphor of my art. We understand each other in the non-verbal language of images, since the point of the images is to show all that which escapes conceptualisation.

MAGDALENA ABAKANOWICZ
September 1994

Shimon Attie
Born USA 1957.
Since the early 1990s, has divided his time between Berlin and San Francisco.

See *Shimon Attie: Photographs and Installations*, Edition Braus, Heidelberg, 1994.

INTRODUCTION
After finishing art school in San Francisco, I came to Berlin in the summer of 1991. Walking the streets of the city that summer, I felt myself asking over and over again, Where are all the missing people? What has become of the Jewish culture and community which had once been at home here? I felt the presence of this lost community very strongly, even though so few visible traces of it remained.

The Writing on the Wall grew out of my response to the discrepancy between what I felt and what I did not see. I wanted to give this invisible past a voice, to bring it to light, if only for some brief moments.

THE WRITING ON THE WALL PROJECT
For this project, I slide-projected portions of pre-Second World War photographs of Jewish street life in Berlin on to the same or nearby locations today. These projections were on view for

one or two evenings, and were visible to neighbourhood residents, street traffic, and passers-by. By using slide projection on-location, fragments of the past were introduced into the visual field of the present. Thus, parts of long-destroyed Jewish community life were visually simulated, momentarily re-created. By attempting to renegotiate the relationship between past and present events, the aim of the project was to interrupt the collective processes of denial and forgetting.

During the course of the projections I would photograph the installations. The photographic exposures were three to four minutes in duration, long enough to sometimes capture a passing car or bicycle. The Writing on the Wall project exists both as on-location installations or performances, as well as fine art photographs. While the installations are long gone, it is my hope and intention that the images from the project go beyond being simply records of the past projections, but have a life and power of their own.

THE SCHEUNENVIERTEL

The Writing on the Wall project took place in the Scheunenviertel neighbourhood in the eastern part of Berlin, near Alexanderplatz. In the early part of this century, the Scheunenviertel had been the quarter of the Jewish working class. The area teemed with Ostjuden, Russian and Polish Jewish immigrants who had come from the East to settle in Berlin in the early part of the twentieth century. The Jews of the Scheunenviertel did not readily assimilate, unlike their German-Jewish cousins living elsewhere in Berlin. They continued to dress as they had in the shtetl, keeping their beards, forelocks, long coats and fur-trimmed hats. Their storefronts bore signs in Hebrew and Yiddish. Their Jewishness was highly visible, a fact reflected in the pre-war photographs taken in this quarter, and this quarter alone. Such images became the basis for the project.

THE PROJECTIONS

After assembling photographs for the project, I had to locate pre-war maps, as the East German government had renamed and renumbered many of the streets after the war. Walking with photographs in one hand and pre-war maps in the other, I first attempted to match up the pictures with the actual sites that had been photographed sixty years ago. Much to my initial disappointment, I discovered that most of the original buildings had been either bombed during the war or torn down, to be rebuilt in the 'mass-produced' style of the so-called Plattenbauten, common during the socialist regime. I quickly discovered that in order to realise this project, I would have to respond to the Scheunenviertel as it exists today. When it was not possible to project on to the original architecture, the projections were made on to neighbouring buildings. I did, however, make every effort to project an image on to its original site, which was possible in about twenty-five per cent of the installations.

During the year I worked on the project, the reactions of local residents to the projections changed dramatically. At first, most people responded positively with curiosity or outright fascination. One gentleman in his fifties responded quite emotionally, telling me that his Jewish grandfather, whom he had never known, had been deported to Auschwitz. On another occasion, a teenage boy involved with a German-Israeli friendship group spontaneously offered to help and kept me company for a few evenings.

But as the year progressed and as economic conditions in East Berlin deteriorated, reactions grew aggressive and hostile. One man, seeing a projection on his building, called the police, protesting that his neighbours would think he was Jewish. Another man shouted down from his fifth-floor apartment, ordering me to stop my projections on a building across the street, and threatening to douse me and my equipment with water if I didn't. I ignored him and continued. He did indeed pour the water, shouting 'Wessie, go home!' He couldn't have known, of course, that I lived in the Scheunenviertel at the time.

Towards the final three months of the project, the situation in East Berlin had begun to worsen to the point where I was harassed and threatened in some way almost every evening by someone who was often, but not always, drunk. I was relieved to finish my work when I did. I would not feel safe doing such a project today, at least not on my own.

SHIMON ATTIE
September 1994

Christian Boltanski
Born France 1944, of a Jewish father and Christian mother. Lives and works in Paris.

See *Christian Boltanski: Lessons of Darkness*, Israel Museum, Jerusalem, 1989; and Gumpert, Lynn, *Christian Boltanski*, Flammarion, Paris, 1994.

Q: Do you consider yourself Jewish?

Yes, I chose to be a Jew at the age of four, under the strangest of circumstances, though it wasn't entirely a matter of choice. Actually I'm a Corsican; my mother was a Corsican, a passionate woman, extremely intelligent, a writer. She was unable to walk, since as a child she had contracted infantile paralysis. It's interesting that she of all people brought us closer to Judaism, since she wasn't afraid of it; Judaism did not pose a threat to her. She herself came from a good French family. The reason I chose to be a Jew as opposed to a Corsican is because I was born to an 'unknown mother'. The first to recognise me was my Jewish father, in other words, 'I chose him'.

I was born while my parents were divorced. In order to save my father's life, they staged a fight and afterwards divorced officially. My mother then hid my father underneath the floor of our house for the duration of the war. I was born on the day Paris was liberated; my mother couldn't go out to register my birth since there was still shooting in the streets. So the first time my father came out of hiding was when he went to give notice of my birth at the municipality. He registered me as a son without a mother, I mean, the son of an unknown mother, and she only recognised me a year after my birth, when they had remarried.

I chose Judaism, which is a privilege most people don't enjoy since unfortunately, for most Jews it's not a matter of choice. Choosing to be a Jew was certainly the most important event of my life …

147

I think there's a strong Jewish component to my work. I have always dealt with the concept of memory, which I'm sure is a Jewish characteristic. The Jews speak of a world which has disappeared, so memory plays an important role for them. The notion of a previously existing world has always been around. The search for this lost ideal world is undoubtedly related to Judaism …

[Interviewer: Bracha Ettinger]
From *Christian Boltanski: Lessons of Darkness*, Israel Museum, Jerusalem, 1989.

Daisy Brand
Born Czechoslovakia 1929. Survived numerous camps, including Auschwitz.
Emigrated to USA in 1966. Lives and works in Boston.

One of the principles underlying my work is the wish to give testimony to an era, and communicate an experience that is totally unique in history and which I was a part of.

I have been interested in drawing since early childhood. After the Second World War, as a teen-age survivor of the Holocaust, I had no opportunity to pursue art, while trying to grow up on my own, and survive in post-war Czechoslovakia. Much later, when life became more stable, at age thirty-two I enrolled in art school, majoring in ceramics. For years I worked in various techniques in clay, making functional pottery, teaching and turning to sculptural forms in my private time, where I could better express my personal concerns. Gradually expressions of my Holocaust experiences started to penetrate this work in the early 1980s.

My references are suggestive and deliberately ambiguous. I try to keep the exact meaning of some of the symbolism in my work private, and I hope to evoke an emotional response in the viewer to the power and meaning of that symbolism, which I believe is universal as well as personal.

The materials I work with, namely porcelain as well as other clays, undergo a dramatic metamorphosis from soft, smooth, almost sensual, to hard and resilient. To bring about this metamorphosis, the clay has to go through intense heat, radiating an orange glow from the cracks of the kiln, not unlike the crematoria in the night sky of Auschwitz. In my use of colours I allude to this analogy. The process in clay work is as old as civilisation itself. Somehow the fascination for me is that fire in this case creates, rather than destroys, which I hope to apply to my life as well.

DAISY BRAND
October 1994

Melvin Charney
Born Canada 1935.
Lives and works in Montreal.

See *Parables and Other Allegories: The Work of Melvin Charney 1975-1990*, Canadian Centre for Architecture, Montreal, 1991.

In 1980, during a visit to Germany at the invitation of the

Deutscher Werkbund, I came across the ruins of a bombed-out factory outside Frankfurt. At the base of a massive brick chimney were the remains of several large furnaces with rusted doors askew … The spectre of the death camps rushed to my mind, as it did for my German host. How could it be otherwise?

A year later, I was asked to submit a proposal for a temporary installation to be built in Kassel for an exhibition called Documenta Urbana that was to be part of Documenta 7. The intention was to draw Documenta 7 out of the confines of the museum precinct and into the city. Several sites were suggested. I found myself working on the Bahnhofplatz, a square that is no more than an ill-defined open area surrounded by a disparate collection of glass-sheathed buildings, all of which emerged out of the ruins of a city heavily bombed during the war – Kassel was an important railroad junction. The Bahnhofplatz drew me to another well-known place of arrival by train, to the railway entrance to Auschwitz-Birkenau conceived by SS architects in the form of an idealised gatehouse to a farm estate. I proposed a reconstruction of the Auschwitz-Birkenau railway entrance in the Bahnhofplatz, opposite the existing railway station; that is, the placement of a critical place of arrival in the place of arrival, one Bahnhof to be reflected in the façade of another Bahnhof.

The figure of this infamous gatehouse is fixed in our consciousness. And if we are to come to terms with its history, then the salient indices ingrained in the representation of the 'worst of all camps' have to be laid bare. The railroad entrance to Auschwitz-Birkenau was made to appear innocent, but this innocence was part of the malevolent cover-up devised by the architects of the Final Solution to hide their killing machine from their victims and to conceal it from the world: 'better if they think that they are going to a farm …'.

The city administration objected to my proposal. A photomontage of the installation was removed from an exhibition of projects for Documenta Urbana. I then suggested a second version of this piece, to be located on a main street leading to the centre of Kassel. On one side of this street are three-storey flats typical of post-war Volk architecture, on the other side are rows of modern office buildings housing the 'economic miracle', and, in between, the rails of a tramway line. Here, perpendicular to the street, I again proposed to install the entrance to Auschwitz-Birkenau, its main arch to be centred on the existing tramway rail line as in the extermination camp. This superimposition disengaged formative layers in what appeared to be an ordinary street – a medieval portico that demarcated the Nazi ideal of the historic core of a German city appeared, as did images of the tramway lines that traversed the walls of Jewish ghettos transporting Übermenschen through the cages of 'puppets' condemned to death. The installation was never built. Documenta Urbana floundered on the political and aesthetic shoals of Documenta 7.

In subsequent work, I attempted to examine the inner structure of the extermination camps. I drew and re-drew the lines of barracks, the crematoria and chimneys, to make visible a force hidden by appearances. The distribution of arrival ramps and watchtowers, the grid of the barrack compounds, the stable-barracks stacked with body racks that reach deep into the earth, the sanitary gas chambers, the encumbered crematoria ovens innovated by Topf engineers, the ever present chimneys; all part of a well-orchestrated machine, its twisted logic defying the boundaries of comprehension.

It was also important for me to fit together the pieces of the camp, to constitute the entity within which each building-chimney, each barrack-crematorium, relates to the other. The structure of a city is evident in the tightly organised plan of Auschwitz-Birkenau. And as with all cities, this city, albeit a city of death, the counterpart of cities that sustain life, has a history. This history is one that closes in on itself, but it was long in the making.

What began in my work with an attempt to grasp the pervasive image of the death camps, culminated in a relevation. The outline of an extermination camp appeared in a reconstruction of Ezekiel's Temple of Jerusalem, as interpreted by a seventeenth-century Lutheran theologian. This appropriation of the Temple usurped, again, a Jewish symbol of regeneration; and, again, the Jews were banished from Jerusalem. Three hundred years later, this purged model of the Celestial City can be seen to prefigure an earth-bound city of death.

MELVIN CHARNEY
November 1994

Deborah Davidson
Born USA 1950.
Lives and works in Boston.

Trace – indication, fragment, taste, shred, shade, shadow, nuance, suggestion, touch, proof, rundown, hunt, ascertain, investigate, pursue.

My interest in my family history has coincided with the making of artists' books. The work is a way of asking questions, a way of remembering, and a way of paying homage. It leads me not only to the investigation of my personal relationship to the past, but also to dealing with the larger historical and cultural issues of being Jewish in society; to events that have caused disruption and dispersion, whether it is 1492, 1944 or 1995. My maternal side is of Sephardic extraction. The work here, Trace, is based on the matrix of a family tree that traces the Servadios from the fourteenth century. In a previous book, entitled Family Tree, I imagined the movement of the family from the time of the Inquisition in Spain to the present, to myself. Although based on facts, the book is poetic in every sense. I began researching the history of the Sephardic Jews and of the Jews in Italy. Trace is a response to the start of this research. Part of my inquiry took the form of a visit to Italy, where I visited many relatives, visited cemeteries, spent time listening to stories. I am tirelessly interested in hearing family stories; not only do I need to hear them again, but I am interested in their variations. In my work, I am participating in the telling, and retelling.

Like many of my other pieces, Trace has been produced by layering imagery, so that things are revealed and concealed at the same time. It is made of ninety-five pages measuring nine by eleven inches. They are inextricably bound by knots that act as hinges, in five vertical 'chapters'. Small folios are sewn into

fifteen of the surrounding pages, which reiterate the overlapping tree-like forms of the larger pages. The text is scattered throughout the images, almost arbitrarily assigned to a page; in this way, these phrases and musings can be 'read' with various meanings. The surrounding neutral sheets contain the epitaph written in memoriam to the Jews of Turin who died in the Holocaust, among them my great-grandmother and her mother. This event is the central wound in my history. Trace then becomes a conduit, a leap of faith. It is a way of tracing memory and history, of making visible that which is evanescent.

DEBORAH DAVIDSON
September 1994

John Goto
Born Manchester 1949.
Lives and works in Oxford.

See Goto, John, Terezin, Wadham Ante Chapel/Cambridge Darkroom/John Hansard Gallery, Southampton, 1988.

REMBRANDT IN TEREZIN
In the Sonderwerkstätte [special workshop] at Terezin, copies of paintings by Rembrandt were made for the Nazi authorities. The lower right-hand image is after a drawing by Terezin artist Dr Karel Fleischmann entitled First Night of New Arrivals. The photograph shows Jews at the Trade Fair grounds in Holesvoice, a suburb of Prague, assembling for deportation to Terezin [1942].

Sally Heywood
Born Liverpool 1964.
Has lived in Berlin since 1990.

Many people remembered the Synagogue as it had been, some were Jewish and had returned to the area. I was able to learn the whole history of Monbijou almost on the street and I built a relationship to this building that became extremely important to me.

My aim was not only to produce a documentation of the rebuilding, I wanted to use the Synagogue as a symbol for Berlin today.

The Synagogue symbolises for me both destruction and reconstruction on a wider scale. It is in itself politically important – the rebuilding plans were instigated under the Honecker regime – and it stands for a new era, in German opinion.

My strongest impression of the rebuilding progress was one evening towards the end of winter 1991. They had started working, inside the building and against the evening light I was aware of a deep red that came from inside. It gave me the distinct impression of a burning. Shortly afterwards I was given a photograph of 'Pogrom Nacht' [of November 1938].

Perhaps a warning or an ironic glimpse when set against the facts of the new Germany. Germany today has still its racist problems, the attacks on foreigners increase daily. The synagogue itself has to have a twenty-four-hour police guard and there have been attacks on the headquarters of the 'Jüdische Gemeinde'.

My impression is also that the Germans are afraid to confront their own history. One encounters both reticence and hostility when one tries to raise this issue. It is clear that many Germans want to forget and wipe away the memories.

As an artist I was compelled to work in some way in this direction. Each artist has his/her own experience to bring into form. I could certainly not have produced such work in England.

My thoughts on the Holocaust have been considerably changed since my time in Berlin. It is difficult to comprehend when one lives outside of the event and time, and it is also easy to forget the unpalatable events of history. But I believe the spirits of people and events do not die out so quickly, they exist for me here in the middle of Berlin and existed for me also in Theresienstadt.

I believe as an artist that I have a responsibility so to work because I am in the position to do so. For me Berlin was personified by the Synagogue. The Holocaust is German history and unquestionably the worst event this century. It should not be allowed to be forgotten.

I have the feeling that it is starting to be whitewashed. The significance of the Synagogue being rebuilt was not overwhelming for the Germans.

Christo wanting to wrap up the Reichstag was, however, big news.

SALLY HEYWOOD
September 1994

R. B. Kitaj

Born USA 1932.
Has lived in England since late 1950s.

See Kitaj, R.B., *First Diasporist Manifesto*, Thames & Hudson, London, 1989; and Livingstone, Marco, *Kitaj*, Phaidon, London, 1992.

… Ours was a household full of secular Diasporists who seemed to be Jews only by the way. It would be many more years before I learned that the Germans and Austrians who did what they did in that time, when I was playing baseball and cruising girls, made no distinction between Believers or atheists or the one and a half million Jewish infants who went up in smoke. One third of all Jews on earth were murdered in my youth.

… That's what I want to be, a tribal remembrancer, wrestling with my Diasporic angel.

… Jews do not own the Diaspora; they are not the only Diasporists by a long shot. They are merely mine.

… My case is built on a cliché which may also be an insightful art lesson. It is that the threatened condition of the Jews witnesses the condition of our wider world. It is a radical witness.

… Forever and a day, and long after Adorno (1903-69), people will argue whether or not 'art' can or should touch upon the Shoah. The fact is that no one can touch anything but its shadow, which lies across the path of some of us, however indistinct. Like most people, I only know the shadow, its aspect in my life … In the lives of those who were there, the shadows,

their shadows are not indistinct at all. They are called memories. It feels very strange/awful/awe-full to be alive, still, in the stinking aftermath of the Shoah, to know people who were there during that time. Giotto and Michelangelo and Rembrandt knew their Passion, its central locus in their lives, more than a thousand years after the event. In the studio, what can be said? What can be faced? I think I know (for the moment). It is what the splendid R. P. Blackmur (1904-65) called 'the radical imperfection of the intellect striking on the radical imperfection of the imagination'.

From R. B. Kitaj, *First Diasporist Manifesto*, Thames and Hudson, 1989.

Kitty Klaidman

Born Czechoslovakia 1937. Survived the war in hiding.
Lives and works in Washington DC.

Somehow, it seems to take about forty years for survivors to come to terms with their personal Holocaust experiences. It took me just over forty years to return to the places in western Slovakia where I was hidden as a child. Ever since that trip I have been working out my feelings about this part of my past through images on paper and canvas. The first paintings were sombre renderings of the forests surrounding our home town not far from Bratislava, the Slovak capital. We escaped at night through these dense woods to a tiny farm village where we were hidden for the last year of the war. Ever since then I have felt ambivalent about the woods – something threatening and hostile on the one hand, something womb-like and nurturing on the other.

The next group of paintings, which are represented in this exhibition, depict the dark hiding places in which I was confined – and saved – with my parents and brother. In each of these works I have introduced a seemingly paradoxical infusion of light, which may represent the remarkable reality that my immediate family survived intact. What it surely represents, however, is that the existence of people like Jan Velicky, the man most responsible for saving us, serves as a beacon of hope in the most desperate times. For me, being able to confront these spaces, as they are now and as I remember them, made me realise the extent to which I have made peace with my past.

I have left the spaces empty to emphasise their neutrality, the fact that they are defined architectonically for the banal purpose of storing inanimate goods. That they were used, by an act of will, an act of courage, to save human lives, is the emotional negative space that defines these paintings. For me the beams, the rafters, the floorboards, the emptiness, are resonant with fear and hope, with hate and love. The odd, somewhat unnatural fusion of darkness and light is my attempt to revivify memory, to give it structure, to understand it. The work in this exhibition did not complete the cycle in which I sought to come to grips with my childhood memories, but it helped me define the meaning of my experience and it enabled me to go on to work that is more intimate.

The next group of images I made are intensely personal. They are mixed-media works incorporating Xerox copies of old photographs of my family, the people who saved us, and the places where we lived and were hidden. I have also used new photographs my children and I took on our trip. The physical act of handling these photographs, collaging them on to canvas, painting on them and framing them in halos of metallic acrylic, was genuinely cathartic for me. There is also something symbolically distancing in converting photographs into Xerox copies and then absorbing them into a work of art. They represent our pre-war life, the journey into hiding, and the period in which we were actually hidden, during which the constant strength of my parents kept us from despair.

The last work in the cycle returns to the architectural spaces represented in the current exhibition, and renders them abstractly, thereby further distancing me from my most haunting and oppressive memories.

KITTY KLAIDMAN
September 1994

Henning Langenheim
Born Hamburg, Germany, 1950.
Since 1970 has lived and worked in Berlin.

ON MY WORK
When I was a small boy my aunts would occasionally take me on exciting trips into the centre of Hamburg. We would inevitably pass a large square memorial carved with rows of marching soldiers, their weapons shouldered. An inscription set over their grim robotic faces read: 'Germany shall live even if we have to die.'

I'd been living in Berlin for quite some time when the excavations began on the Autodrom, a strange site on the western side of the notorious Wilhelmstrasse, the former centre of government cut in two by the Berlin Wall. On this wasteland, between heaps of dumped construction rubble, people could drive old cars without a licence.

The excavations revealed the torture cells of the 'Reichssicherheits-hauptamt', the headquarters of terror in Nazi-occupied Europe. My ignorance of the existence of this place, where the unthinkable had been organised and carried out, shocked me.

At that time Claude Lanzmann's film Shoah *was screened in a fringe show of the Berlin Film Festival. I found myself wondering how memory was made visible at all the places that had once belonged, in one way or another, to this universe of terror controlled from what Berliners today call the Gestapo-site.*

Since then, in my travels through Europe and Israel, I have visited some seventy official and unofficial memorial sites in eleven countries: remains of camps, mass graves, ghettos, synagogues and cemeteries.

I have seen the switch at Oswiecim rail station, where the death trains left the main track into the huge death factory at Auschwitz-Birkenau, and the steps which led the victims down to the undressing rooms of the big gas chambers. Their spoons still lie scattered on the ground, rusted by decades of rain.

I have seen fragments of human bone and ash mingled in the earth of the tiny compound of Belzec death camp. Through a window set in a small hill overgrown with grass at Sobibor I have seen buried ashes and a single skull.

At the sites of the big concentration camps in East and West Germany there was often little left to see save well-tended grass. Most of the remains of these places of terror were removed before the sites were transformed into places of commemoration. Instead, reconstructions and museum displays try to evoke the horrors of the past.

Nothing was impossible during my journeys: village children and dogs playing with skulls and bones between the broken graves of a Jewish cemetery; a synagogue used as a public swimming pool; violent, anti-Semitic slogans written in German on mass graves some one thousand miles east of Germany.

Later, after the fall of the Wall, I travelled further east into the countries of the former Soviet Union. I saw rubbish heaps on unmarked mass graves, and redundant Soviet memorials dumped on the grounds of an annihilation camp.

I met Jewish survivors living in poverty, who hadn't yet seen a penny from the German government. Once a year they rent the city's theatre, a former synagogue, to celebrate Yom Kippur.

I spent a day searching for an execution site where several thousand people were killed in a remote area on the shores of the Baltic Sea. When I finally got there, with the help of an army major, my camera did not know what to photograph after a thousand miles of travel: the grass, the sand, the big sky.

Now, when I return to Hamburg, I find the soldiers' memorial confronted by another: a memorial by the Austrian artist Alfred Hrdlicka to the victims of the Neuengamme concentration camp just outside Hamburg. The dying prisoners seem to fall on the confused shoppers passing by. Often both memorials are covered in graffiti. Sometimes they are cleaned. A controversy has raged for years over whether one or both of them should be removed to a less central place.

As I write this in the autumn of 1994 the German government is making plans to erect a memorial to the victims of the Holocaust on Potsdamer Platz in Berlin. Whatever the result of the architectural competition, for me the real memorials are those scattered sites where the mass murder was carried out: grass, sand, ashes, some stones, concrete blocks.

And when I look through these photographs of places thousands of miles apart from each other, they seem to form a composite view of the ways in which the German mass murder is remembered today.

HENNING LANGENHEIM
October 1994

Lena Liv
Born Russia 1952. Moved to Israel in 1976.
Since c.1980 has divided her time between Israel and Italy.

See *Lena Liv*, Leopold-Hoesch-Museum, Duren/Heidelberger Kunstverein, 1990; *Lena Liv*, Galerie Reckermann, Cologne, 1992; and *Lena Liv: Die Stille der Dinge*, Städtische Galerie Würzburg 1994.

Human history drips with horrors; but the Nazi Holocaust has its own special form of horror.

Conceived in the Europe of Kant, Mozart and Schopenhauer, the Holocaust was consummated as a devastating, uncontainable ritual, scientifically organised for the destruction of a whole value system. The Holocaust denies pietas and identifies anyone 'different' as a cancerous cell in the social body, to be not just extirpated, but extirpated with revulsion. That stolid revulsion, against which there is no appeal, kills the 'different', even more than physical death does.

I was brought up in the memory of the Holocaust, and I think that not just for Jews but for every human creature who becomes aware of it, the Holocaust can turn into an incurable break between the individual and humanity. I believe this is a contributory determinant of the sense of infinite dismay, of coldness and pain, that I feel, even if rarely and despite myself, welling up from the unconscious. In any case, over and above possible traumas in the unconscious, for me the Nazi Holocaust heightens perception of the 'sense of finality' of death and of things lost in the silence and darkness of time. It is just in this silence of things lost that I am working, where the heritage of the Holocaust flows together with the heritage of universal pain: pain at the fate of things that 'because they are' (Anaximander's terrible insight) must repay the 'guilt of being' according to 'time's decree'. What I feel now is that the 'must' of my work is the recovery of the image of 'things as they were in themselves', so as to be able, in the pietas of memory, to save them from 'time's decree'. And I believe that the photographic image (when in particular circumstances it grasps the 'essence' of things) is the most immediate and tragic indication of things in themselves and of the human soul (in the human portraits). Above all, I believe that the photographic image, by fixing the 'instantaneous time' of things, brings out the existence of the 'arrow of time' against which philosophy and science have always been measuring themselves, especially in relation to death.

Photography in my work meets other raw materials: handmade paper and iron (wrought or cast). Making the paper by hand gives consistency to objects of lost reality, in a metamorphosis between memory and matter that enables me to realise the memory image in three dimensions too. This technique of reproducing three-dimensional images in hand-made coloured paper remains an essential feature of my researches, along with the 'recovery' of photographic images as a sorcery for withdrawing them from the reality of time. Acting as a frame for the photographic images and the 'metamorphic' function of 'paper as material' (and thus for its total fragility) is wrought or cast iron, mute testimony to the force of 'reality' against the arrow of time.

However, I do not look for special conceptual meanings in the use of these media (photographic image, objects in paper, iron), even though I am well aware that media always have an intrinsic significance of their own.

Using them is a response to the attempt to materialise the 'feel' of lost things, a feeling that emerges from the image of things.

And since the meaning of things is largely ineffable, in the survival of the image it is above all the mystery of things that survives; and this is perhaps all it remains possible to save from oblivion, time's Holocaust.

LENA LIV
November 1994

Fabio Mauri
Born Bologna, 1926, into aristocratic Italian family.
Lives and works in Rome.

See *Fabio Mauri: Opere e Azioni 1954-1994*, Galleria Nazionale d'Arte Moderna, Rome 1994.

THE WESTERN OR WAILING WALL
Confronting once again an early exhibition, Ebrea (1971), like an old piece of luggage which has been closed for a long time, I immediately realised that it was disquietingly topical.

Racism is as present in the West today as it was before, and is even more widespread. It operates as an extreme search for identity, or as a determination to settle old scores once and for all. To start afresh, blanking out the interlocutor, following a hypothesis of reality so independent from the course of events, seems like a settling of old debts and claims, like the Wars of the Roses; it appears, and indeed perhaps is, beyond any history.

What anguish, blindness, death and narrow-mindedness this Western neurosis involves can easily be verified daily in reports in the Mediterranean and Oceanic press.

Poetry makes diagnoses and comparisons, and when it can it passes judgements and composes expressive and effective metaphors. It can affect the course of events, at least predictively. It is not first aid, but deep intellectual succour, entrusted to time in the solid completeness of its linguistic formulation.

The Western Wall, or Wailing Wall, as the remaining wall of King Solomon's Temple is known, is reconstructed here out of suitcases. This is an attempt to represent that necessary wall of ideals and faith, of yearning for goodness, amongst all the luggage in transit, luggage forced into exile, forced to search for identity, or carrying incinerated and uprooted identities. It is a construction of different origins, which stands on its own, with no other support than its own, necessary, human complexity. Soft and hard materials, cardboard, wood and leather are the stones of this wall, a self-supporting collage.

I have been told that at Auschwitz one of the most striking documents is a heap of suitcases. Each one carries, in the name written on its label, the certainty of a return. Here the connection with the installation/performance entitled Ebrea becomes manifest.

In the inner part of the exhibition space the Wall is flat, like a true wall, but it is detached and has uneven blocks on its outside face, evoking contemporary patterns of transmigration. For a number of different reasons, these blocks appear to be too enigmatic to be deciphered or arranged as a whole with adequate objectivity and precision.

Jews poke small pieces of paper containing their prayers to God in the gaps in the Wailing Wall. These are concerned with the soul, with loved-ones, the body and worldly life.

I have made a symbol for them with a single roll of cloth. This is a prayer in art. The Jews say that the wall is the place where God will always listen, and so I have assumed it to be. It is a place of value therefore.

There is also a plant growing, a sign of the life that the dead or square blocks of stone, or the empty and inert suitcases, are incapable of hindering.

FABIO MAURI
May 1994

Zoran Music

Born Slovenia 1909. A non-Jew, he was incarcerated in Dachau for his Resistance activities.
Lives and works in Paris and Venice.

See *Zoran Music*, Accademia di Francia a Roma, Villa Medici, Rome/Electa, Milan, 1992.

We lived in a world that was beyond all imagining, a world which was absurd, hallucinating, unreal: another planet, maybe. There were strange rules, a precise and cruel order, at the limit of what could even be believed. Anyone invested with the slightest bit of authority, no matter how small, could crush you like a worm. And you accepted this reality, as though there could not possibly exist a different order of things. You even came to fear the outside world.

… I drew in a state of frenzy, morbidly clutching my scraps of paper to me. I was dazzled by the hallucinating grandeur of these fields of corpses. And as I drew I would grasp a thousand details. What tragic elegance there was in those frail bodies, in details so precise: in the hands, the thin fingers, the feet; and in the mouths too, half open in a final attempt to catch one more breath of air; and in the bones covered with pale skin, barely touched with blue. I was haunted by the desire not to betray these diminished forms, to render them, as precious as I saw them, reduced to bare essentials. And I felt the irresistible urge to draw, so that this tremendous and tragic beauty might not escape me.

… I had these mounds of corpses in my mind's eye; and later, when I discovered these hills around Siena, ravaged by wind and rain, those clay features, stripped down by the weather and looking like skeletons barely covered with skin, I felt a shock: for in them I recognised the mounds of the dead and dying in the camp.

… In this tremendous sum of tragedies, in all of these facts which were so utterly tragic, there was also an extreme beauty which resided, as I have said, in all the little details, such as the thin-fingered hands of the dead. And also, you came to realise in such moments that once you have taken away all a man's insignia of function, all his decorations, when his head has been shaved and even his moustache, and he has been stripped of every outward index of importance, what remains is really what you are. And then you begin to wonder: what am I really? And all men become alike – there is no distance left between a bishop, a minister of state or a tramp.

… When we were there in the camp, people would often declare that this sort of thing could never happen again. When the war is over, they said, a better world will come into being, and such horrors will never recur … But then, as time went by, I saw the same thing starting to happen again all over the world: in Vietnam, in the Gulag, in Latin America – everywhere. And I realised that what we had said in those days – that we would be the last people to experience such things – was not true: the truth is that we were not the last.

… The experience I had in Dachau helped me to get down to essentials – to eliminate everything that was not indispensable. And today too, I want to paint with a minimum of means. In these works of mine, there is no more gesturing, no more violence. You attain a kind of silence which may be a characteristic of my work. For in the death of all these people at Dachau, you see, there was never anything rhetorical. In the thousands of deaths I witnessed there, I never heard a single outcry, never saw even a gesture of protest. And of course protest itself was quite unthinkable in such circumstances. All that comes out in my paintings. And so I am quite incapable, after all I have gone through, of carrying on in a demagogical, rhetorical way, as do all those who find a polemical situation to their advantage. I have lived in a world that was utterly tragic, and I discovered that this was a place where silence reigned. It was the contrary of all one might have expected. And the tragedy became much greater and more intense because of this.

Quoted in Michael Gibson, 'Tua Res Agitur', in *Zoran Music: We Are Not the Last*, Virgin Islands, 1988.

Natan Nuchi

Born Israel 1951, the child of a Holocaust survivor.
Lives and works in New York.

See *Natan Nuchi: Paintings*, Museum of Modern Art, Haifa, Israel, 1992.

In the early 1980s, I began making paintings with figures that reminded me of concentration camp inmates. The Holocaust meant for me an authentic, primal realm, that as subject matter for art defied prevalent trends of ironical and tongue-in-cheek preoccupation with appropriation and inauthenticity. The photographic imagery from the Holocaust seemed to me to be among the most extreme in the pool of images that exist in our culture and once I became aware of the Holocaust, I felt that in my own search for the authentic in art I had to keep some kind of eye contact with it.

The photographic images of the naked, bald and emaciated figures represent for me at once the most private and the most political. The nakedness and the emaciation point to the intimacies, vulnerabilities and biological terminality of the individual. But the same nakedness, emaciation and baldness point also to the violence and suffering inflicted on the individual by politics, by society, and by history.

Being an Israeli Jew and son of a survivor may account in part for the way the Holocaust is reflected in my work. While the memory of the Holocaust is often related as a story of survivors and rescuers, heroes and martyrs, for me the victims are the essence of the Holocaust. My most immediate and most enduring reaction to it is an emotional one. Empathy and the many feelings it triggers are the source of the need I have felt to be involved with the subject.

In approaching the Holocaust or alluding to it, I have had to contend with the morality of using the suffering of others to make art and the relevance of making paintings in relation to existing photographs. But in time I have decided that the vitality of the memory of the Holocaust depends on the possibility of renewal, and metaphorically speaking, I saw my paintings as commentary and the photographs as the scriptures. I believe that paintings, at their best, have the ability to externalise feeling and reveal an existential layer that is not apparent in most photographs and I also believe that art can fuse and absorb the documentary materials – the visual and literary – and open up an emotional and intellectual relation to the Holocaust that documentation does not allow.

The large-scale image of the single, naked, bald and emaciated figure, particularly the white-skinned powerless male, goes against consumeristic and capitalistic ideals of optimism, activism and the attainment of power. In this context my art points also to our culture's difficulty with the Holocaust and the constant need it has to subvert and reshape the Holocaust's meaning to fit its own ideals. Mortality, vulnerability and being victimised are either repressed or kept in low profile, and can be generally tolerated in the art of this society, only if the aesthetic pleasure, such as beauty of form, richness of texture and material, etc. can surpass the harshness and pain of the subject matter. Regardless of quality, most of the art that becomes acceptable in our society, and ultimately is shown in our museums, has much to do with what initially the patrons of art find suitable to hang on their living room walls. It seems to me that for art to be congenial to living room surroundings and be in any meaningful way reflective of the horror and extreme experience of the Holocaust, is an impossibility, a failure or a contradiction that may ultimately cause us either to change our awareness of the Holocaust or our expectations of art.

I believe that the problem of how not to dilute and domesticate the harshness of the Holocaust by too much restraint, symbols, metaphors or recognisable icons on the one hand, and how not to participate in a crude 'horror show' on the other, will render no artist's achievement free from some measure of failure. But there is a redeeming value to art that deals with the subject: the same qualities that threaten to trivialise the Holocaust and often do, might also be the qualities that help us – artists and viewers – enter the subject. The seductive powers of art, its beauty, sensuality and form, draw us in, holding our gaze and retaining our interest in a subject from which we might otherwise have averted our eyes.

NATAN NUCHI
September 1994

Susanna Pieratzki
Born Germany 1965, the child of two Holocaust survivors.
Lives and works in Munich.

PARENTS (1990)
Parents portrays my own parents who, by a stroke of fate, survived the Holocaust. However, this set of photographs does not deal with the actual horrors of the Holocaust.

Its main objective is to show the deep-rooted human instinct to survive such dark times. Despite the mental and physical weakness caused by the past, my parents, as well as many others like them, still possess within them this deep, hidden spark to build a new life and bring forth a new generation.

SUSANNA PIERATZKI
October 1994

Mick Rooney
Born Epsom, Surrey, England 1944.
Lives and works in London.

AFTER AUSCHWITZ
In 1988 I had discovered and devoured the complete works of Primo Levi and added them to the rag-bag of the inner-self to lie in disarray with the choirs of dumbstruck voices already therein. I was a child of suburbia, and the beneficiary of an austere peace.

When, in 1948, a voice said 'Look up!' I saw a sky full of aeroplanes droning their way to Berlin where, I was given to understand, much-needed confectionery would be parachuted in for deprived children of that bomb-blackened city.

Later on, the cinema showed flickering black-and white newsreels from 1945, in which gaunt stick-like spectres moved amongst steel, concrete and earth to form a universe of grey bones.

Joe, my soldier uncle, deposited in our home the spoils of war: a rocking horse for me, aluminium saucepans from the Ruhr, an 8mm movie camera, a commando knife, an Iron Cross (2nd class) and a German Mother's Medal (1st class). When held in the hands, these last two objects transported me to a world peopled by steel-helmeted foes and childbearing, flaxen-haired maidens.

Beneath the cross in the Catholic School the Scribes and Pharisees plotted the downfall of Christ. He was called King of the Jews! Why would the Jews kill their King? And who were they? But more to the point, had my classmate's brother killed Koreans?

In Godless Russia – wherever that was – priests were daily facing terrible ordeals. The returned missionaries told us so. Mainland Europe was uncharted territory and was much further away than pink Canada, where the Mounties always got their man. 'Real' evil seeped between the newsprint pages of the American penny-dreadfuls. A man filled a bath with piranha fish and his wife reluctantly got in. At the Saturday morning pictures, Spider Woman had trapped another victim and Flash Gordon was falling, ever falling into the fiery furnace (until next Saturday morning!).

One day I knew that sometime, in the not too distant past, somewhere closer to home than I had ever thought, families, faces taut and anxious, had awaited the sound of the heavy black boot that came at dawn.

THIS IS A TIME OF LIGHTNING WITHOUT THUNDER,
THIS IS A TIME OF UNHEARD VOICES,
OF UNEASY SLEEP AND USELESS VIGILS,
FRIEND, DO NOT FORGET THE DAYS
OF LONG EASY SILENCES,
FRIENDLY NOCTURNAL STREETS,
SERENE MEDITATIONS.
BEFORE THE LEAVES FALL,
BEFORE THE SKY CLOSES AGAIN,
BEFORE WE ARE AWAKENED AGAIN
BY THE FAMILIAR POUNDING OF IRON FOOTSTEPS
IN FRONT OF OUR DOORS. *

The stories now were set in lands inhabited by beings from another time and culture. They were dark and exotic. There were bearded rabbis from Lithuania called the Hassidim and there were alchemists from Cordoba and Ashkenazim and Sephardim. Some lived in shtetls, others in ghettos and one became a sabre-rattling Cossack caught up in pogroms.

The Israel of the 1960s was heady with nationhood. The Jews lived in the land of Israel but the land of Israel was for Israelis. A chance invitation to a Shabbat supper at the home of a rabbi and his family in Jerusalem's Mea Shearim was preceded by a shaking, nodding service in the synagogue and it reminded me that the world of Shalom Aleichem and Isaac Bashevis Singer still held firm. A visit to the Jerusalem monument and museum with its exhibits and its tablets carved with black acid tears, and the eternal flame to the unquenchable memory of the numberless dead, brought me back to the present.

The narrative paintings from 1989 were conceived as a 'direct response' to Levi's writings and to accompany accounts from literature, film and personal journeys. I attempted to use the paint both as pigment and as subject matter and I wanted the subject itself to exist in 'paint-time', that is, in a time neither biblical nor contemporary.

Although I was at once angered, inspired and of course quite impotent in daring to comment on this unimaginable historical episode of Jewish history, I thought that these icons – no matter that they seemed inadequate – might act as paint signs to the continuing presence of man on this earth, as witnessed by Primo Levi as both survivor and creator.

MICK ROONEY
September 1994

* 'Waiting. 2 January 1949', from *The Collected Poems of Primo Levi*, translated by Ruth Feldman and Brian Swann, published Faber & Faber Ltd, 1988.

Ellen Rothenberg
Born USA 1949.
Lives and works in Chicago.

See *Ellen Rothenberg*, Tufts University Art Gallery, Aidekman Arts Center, Medford, Massachusetts, 1994.

NOTES ON 'THE COMBING SHAWL'
The Combing Shawl *is a sculpture from the* Anne Frank Project, *a three-part installation series based on the life and writings of Anne Frank.*[1] *This series is not a documentary por-trait of a person or a time but focuses on contemporary issues through the historical lens of the* Diary. *The installations reflect on the individual identity of Anne Frank, the person behind the myth separated from the accumulated cultural history of the* Diary, *the plays, movies etc. The installations contain objects which require an alternative reading to the way history, artifacts and documents are conventionally considered. Some refer to actual historical artifacts from Anne Frank's life. Others are newly fabricated or 'false' artifacts. By presenting various kinds of documentation, the distinctions between truth and fiction, denial and falsehood, and our assumptions about history become sharply delineated.*

I began working on The Combing Shawl *while living in Berlin. This provided a certain proximity to the events of the Second World War in Europe and enabled me to research historic sites and archives in Germany as well as at the Anne Frank Institute, the Anne Frank Museum, the Netherlands Institute for War Documentation, and the State Forensic Science Laboratory in The Netherlands.*

My intention in creating this work is not that of a historian or documentalist. I speak as an artist, about an experience of the Diary *that is personal and contemporary. However, the archive, the museum and the forensic laboratory, unlikely sites for the aesthetic imagination, are precisely the sites where the issues of identity and its traces meet the limits of representation.*

[1] The Combing Shawl *refers to an item of clothing belonging to Anne Frank: a small silken cape which she wore around her shoulders when combing her hair. It is one of the few personal effects of Anne Frank to survive the war.*

My sculptural work The Combing Shawl *has the text of the* Diary *as 'hair'. Surrounding the text on the floor are combs cast in aluminium, bronze and magnesium bronze. The casting sand and small bits of metal from the casting process remain adhered to the surface of the combs.*

Shirley Samberg
Born USA 1920.
Lives and works in New York.

When asked to write about my sculpture, it is always a dilemma. What to say?

With an artist it is always the material that speaks. When asked to create a stage-set, I started gathering supplies. Burlap was one of the materials. It was very malleable and to me appealing. I had been welding at the time and needed a change. The challenge of using fabric with wood and earth elements appealed to me. The images seemed to spring from sources deep within me that I wasn't aware of. The dark and brooding sculptures took on a life of their own. I worked with a compulsion I didn't know I possessed. One figure emerged after another. Those who saw them were moved by the dark wellspring of grief. Grief for the loss of loved ones. Grief for the Holocaust. Grief for war, poverty and homelessness ... and the list goes on ...

SHIRLEY SAMBERG
September 1994

Nancy Spero
Born USA 1926.
Lives and works in New York.

See *Nancy Spero*, Institute of Contemporary Art, London, 1987; and *Nancy Spero*, Edition Cantz, Stuttgart, 1990.

Erika Hoffmann: Why did you choose a poem by Bertolt Brecht for your work? And why particularly this one?

Nancy Spero: I chose a poem by Bertolt Brecht because of his straightforward, unflinching look at the human condition; the poem's intensity and evocation of the horror of the times: 1934-6 [the dates of the poem] in Nazi Germany. Since the mid-1970s I have depicted mostly images of, and investigated the status of women, I zeroed in on The Jew's Whore *because it voices in unrelenting terms the Nazi sexual sadism directed against having a Jew as a lover.*

EH: How did you find the image of the woman which you have been using already in previous works? What does it mean to you?

NS: I first heard the poem on National Public Radio. A year or so previously Leon [Golub] gave me this photo of a victim of the Gestapo he'd found in a French photo magazine (he frequently finds images for me in doing research for his own work). The photograph is chilling, but if one doesn't know that it was found on a member of the Gestapo it could be perceived as pornographic titillation. She looks ashamed, violated, bound, her head averted, a heavy rope around her neck. Fantasy alludes to reality. It could be porn but it isn't. It's for real.

EH: How did you start this work: with the image or with the text? And is your answer true for all of your works comprising text and images?

NS: When I heard the poem I was greatly moved by its power – and was struck how the photo of the Gestapo victim amplified the poem: degradation, sexual abuse and victimisation of woman.

EH: You use the text to create a certain picture – or would you call it a pictogram? Is the visual impression of the text as important to you as the message?

NS: Image and text are simultaneously and equally important and relevant. The visual impact of the text is as crucial as the figures; both express strong content printed with staccato rhythm, a varied, almost fractured disjunctive look. The images are extensions of the text – in some instances virtual hieroglyphs.

Extracted from Erika Hoffmann's interview with Nancy Spero, 5 March 1991.

List of Works in Exhibition

1 Magdalena Abakanowicz
Backward Seated Figures
1992-3
Bronze
15 figures, each 86-96 cm (34-38 in) high
Marlborough Gallery Inc, New York

2 Shimon Attie
8 colour photographs from *The Writing on the Wall* series:
a *Joachimstrasse 11a, Berlin: Slide projection of Jewish café with patrons (1933)*
b *Joachimstrasse/corner of Auguststrasse, Berlin: Slide projection of Jewish resident (1931)*
c *Mulackstrasse 32, Berlin: Slide projection of Jewish residents and Hebrew reading-room (1931)*
d *Mulackstrasse 37, Berlin: Slide projection of Jewish residents (c.1932)*
e *Steinstrasse 21, Berlin: Slide projection of Jewish-owned pigeon shop (1931)*
f *Joachimstrasse 20, Berlin: Slide projection of Jewish resident, theatre and Torah reading-room (1929-31)*
g *Linienstrasse 137, Berlin: Slide projection of police raid on Jewish residents (1920)*
h *Almstadtstrasse (formerly Grenadierstrasse)/corner of Schendelstrasse, Berlin: Slide projection of religious book salesman (1930)*
All 1991
C-type photographs
Each 50 × 60 cm (19½ × 23½ in)
Zelda Cheatle Gallery, London
(*See Col.Fig.55*)

3 Christian Boltanski
Altar to the Chajes High School
1987
4 b/w photos in metal frames, 88 tin boxes, 4 lamps
2.23 × 2.38 m (7 ft 3 in × 7 ft 9 in)
Israel Museum, Jerusalem
(*Fig.78*)

4 Daisy Brand
Pasul
1986
Porcelain and wood
38 × 61 × 5 cm (15 × 24 × 2 in)
Artist's Collection, Boston, USA

5 Daisy Brand
Towards Camp C
1988
Porcelain and wood
56 × 48 × 7.5 cm (22 × 19 × 3 in)
Artist's Collection, Boston

6 Daisy Brand
The Broken Promise (triptych)
1990
Porcelain, earthenware and wood
84 × 96.5 × 10 cm (33 × 38 × 4 in)
Artist's Collection, Boston
(*Col.Fig.60*)

7 Daisy Brand
Last Trip
1990
Porcelain and wood
84 × 42 × 10 cm (33 × 16½ × 4 in)
Artist's Collection, Boston
(*Col.Fig.61*)

8 Daisy Brand
The Descent
1990
Porcelain, earthenware and wood
96.5 × 54.5 × 10 cm (38 × 21½ × 4 in)
Artist's Collection, Boston

9 Daisy Brand
Epilogue
1994
Porcelain and wood
66 × 47 × 5 cm (26 × 18½ × 2 in)
Artist's Collection, Boston

10 Melvin Charney
Better if they think they are going to a farm ... No.2
1982
Coloured pencil, conté and pastel on wove paper
1.04 × 1.45 m (3 ft 5 in × 4 ft 9 in)
Canada Council Art Bank, Ottawa

11 Melvin Charney
Fragments of the Forgotten City, No.8
1985
Conté and pastel on wove paper
65.5 cm × 1.03 m (2 ft 1½ in × 3 ft 4½ in)
Musée du Quebec

12 Melvin Charney
Fragments of the Forgotten City, No.10
1985
Pastel on wove paper
53.5 × 53.5 cm (21 × 21 in)
Collection of Mr and Mrs Gesta Abols

13 Melvin Charney
Fragments of the Forgotten City, No.12
1985
Conté and pastel on wove paper
65 cm × 1.02 m (2 ft 1½ in × 3 ft 4 in)
Collection of the Bank of Montreal

14 Melvin Charney
Visions of the Temple (after Matthias Haffenreffer's 'Reconstruction of the Temple of Jerusalem', Tübingen, 1631)
1986
Pastel on wove paper
1.01 × 1.54 m (3 ft 4 in × 5 ft)
National Gallery of Canada, Ottawa
(*Col.Fig.72*)

15 Melvin Charney
The Other City - Visions of the Temple No.1
1986
Pastel on wove paper
92 cm × 1.26 m (3 ft × 4 ft 1½ in)
Centre for Canadian Architecture, Montreal

16 Deborah Davidson
Trace
1992
Book installation: monotype, letraset and xerox transfers on handmade paper
4.27 × 1.83 m (14 ft × 6 ft)
Artist's Collection, Boston
(*Col.Fig.70*)

17 John Goto
Rembrandt in Terezin
1983-8
Oil paint on photograph
1.54 × 1.27 m (5 ft × 4 ft 2 in)
Courtesy Jason and Rhodes Gallery, London
(*Col.Fig.65*)

18 Sally Heywood
The Reconstruction of the Synagogue
1991
Oil on canvas
1.6 × 2 m (5 ft 3 in × 6 ft 7 in)
Paton Gallery, London
(*Col.Fig.58*)

19 Sally Heywood
*The Reconstruction of the Synagogue –
Oranienburgerstrasse*
1991
Charcoal on canvas
1.30 × 1.75 m (4 ft 3 in × 5 ft 9 in)
Paton Gallery, London

20 Sally Heywood
The Burning
1993
Oil on canvas
1.90 × 2.50 m (6 ft 3 in × 8 ft 2 in)
Paton Gallery, London
(*Col.Fig.59*)

21 R. B. Kitaj
Passion (1940-5): Writing
1985
Oil on canvas
45.5 × 26.5 cm (18 × 10½ in)
Artist's Collection, London

22 R. B. Kitaj
Passion (1940-5): Girl/Plume
1985
Oil on canvas
56 × 43 cm (22 × 17 in)
Artist's Collection, London
(*See front cover*)

23 R. B. Kitaj
Passion (1940-5): Reading
1985
Oil on canvas
45.5 × 51 cm (18 × 20 in)
Artist's Collection, London

24 R. B. Kitaj
Passion (1940-5): Landscape/Chamber
1985
Oil on canvas
28 × 51 cm (11 × 20 in)
Artist's Collection, London

25 R. B. Kitaj
Passion (1940-5): Varschreibt! After Picasso
1986
Oil on canvas
43 × 24 cm (16½ × 9½ in)
Artist's Collection, London

26 R. B. Kitaj
Yiddish Hamlet (Y. Löwy)
1985
Oil on canvas
1.22 m × 61 cm (4 ft × 2 ft)
Marlborough Fine Art, London
(*Fig.75*)

27 Kitty Klaidman
Hidden Memories: Attic in Humence (triptych)
1991
Acrylic on paper
3.05 × 1.52 m (10 ft × 5 ft)
Artist's Collection, Washington DC, courtesy
of Marsha Mateyka Gallery
(*Col.Fig.62*)

28 Kitty Klaidman
Hidden Memories: Dark Corner with Window
1991
Acrylic on paper
1.02 × 1.52 m (3 ft 4 in × 5 ft)
Artist's Collection, Washington DC, courtesy
of Marsha Mateyka Gallery

29 Kitty Klaidman
Hidden Memories: Trapdoor
1991
Acrylic on paper
1.52 × 1.02 m (5 ft × 3 ft 4 in)
Artist's Collection, Washington DC, courtesy
of Marsha Mateyka Gallery

Cats 30-33 form part of a series entitled
Memorials

30 Henning Langenheim
*Berlin 1987: 'Gestapo Site'/ 'YOU ARE
STANDING'*
b/w photograph
41 × 35 cm (16 × 14 in)
Artist's Collection, Berlin

31 Henning Langenheim
Sobibor 1987: Mass Grave
b/w photograph
41 × 33.5 cm (16 × 13 in)
Artist's Collection, Berlin
(*Fig.77*)

32 Henning Langenheim
Chelmno 1987: Earth of Chelmno
b/w photograph
33 × 40.5 cm (13 × 16 in)
Artist's Collection, Berlin

33 Henning Langenheim
*Auschwitz-Birkenau 1987: Entrance to
Undressing Room of Gas Chamber and
Crematorium II*
b/w photograph
45.5 × 30.5 cm (18 × 12 in)
Artist's Collection, Berlin

34 Henning Langenheim
Dachau 1987: Grass
b/w photograph
30 × 37.5 cm (12 × 14½ in)
Artist's Collection, Berlin
(*Fig.76*)

35 Henning Langenheim
Karczew 1988: Desecrated Jewish Cemetery
b/w photograph
45 × 34 cm (17½ × 13½ in)
Artist's Collection, Berlin

36 Henning Langenheim
Majdanek 1990: Jackets
b/w photograph
42.5 × 33 cm (16½ × 13 in)
Artist's Collection, Berlin

37 Henning Langenheim
Buchenwald 1991: Panorama
b/w photograph
19.5 × 47.5 cm (7½ × 18½ in)
Artist's Collection, Berlin
(*See Frontispiece*)

38 Henning Langenheim
*Maly Trostenets 1993: Demolished Soviet
Memorials on the Site of a Former
Extermination Camp, Near Minsk, Belarus*
b/w photograph
31.5 × 46.5 cm (12½ × 18 in)
Artist's Collection, Berlin

39 Lena Liv
Memoria di Arianna [Memory of Ariadne]
1990
Iron, macrodevelopment of photographic
spectrum, handmade paper, pigment
1.37 m × 88 cm × 15 cm (4 ft 5 in × 2 ft 11 in
× 6 in)
Private collection, Germany

40 Lena Liv
Untitled
1991
Iron, handmade paper, pigment, silicium
sand, photograph
55 × 100 × 27 cm (22 × 39 × 10½ in)
Private collection, Germany

41 Lena Liv
Memoria di nero e blu [Memory of Black and Blue]
1991-2
Iron, macrodevelopment of photographic spectrum, handmade paper, pigment
181 × 87 × 31 cm (71 × 34 × 12 in)
Private collection, Cologne
(*Col.Fig.71*)

42 Lena Liv
Cavallino con Margharite Rose [Horse with Pink Daisies]
1991
Iron, macrodevelopment of photographic spectrum, handmade paper, pigment
70 × 75 × 17 cm (27½ × 29½ × 6½ in)
Private collection, Cologne

43 Fabio Mauri
Western or Wailing Wall
1993
Leather (real suitcases), wood, canvas
4 m × 4 m × 80 cm (13 ft 1½ in × 13 ft 1½ in × 2 ft 7½ in)
Artist's Collection, Rome
(*Col.Fig.67*)

43a Fabio Mauri
Dieser Koffer ist arisch [This Suitcase is Aryan]
1994
Real leather suitcase
1.144 m × 1 m × 56 cm (3 ft 9 in × 5 ft 5 in × 1 ft 10 in)
Janus Avivson Gallery, London

44 Zoran Music
We Are Not the Last
1970
Etching
35 × 52 cm (14 × 20½ in)
Tate Gallery, London

45 Zoran Music
We Are Not the Last
1970
Etching
40 × 56.5 cm (15½ × 22 in)
Tate Gallery, London

46 Zoran Music
We Are Not the Last
1975
Lithograph
66 × 50.5 cm (26 × 20 in)
Tate Gallery, London

47 Zoran Music
We Are Not the Last
1975
Lithograph
66 × 50 cm (26 × 19½ in)
Tate Gallery, London

48 Zoran Music
Untitled
1975
Lithograph
66 × 50.5 cm (26 × 20 in)
Tate Gallery, London

49 Natan Nuchi
Untitled
1989
Acrylic on canvas
H 2.95 m (9 ft 8 in) (hung diagonally)
Artist's Collection, New York

50 Natan Nuchi
Untitled
1990
Acrylic on canvas
2.24 × 1.12 m (7 ft 4 in × 3 ft 8 in)
Artist's Collection, New York

51 Natan Nuchi
Untitled
1991
Acrylic on canvas
2.74 × 1.72 m (9 ft × 5 ft 8 in)
Artist's Collection, New York

52 Susanna Pieratzki
Parents series
1991
a *War*
b *Question*
c *Begin*
d *Love*
e *Money*
f *Birth*
g *Chef*
h *Motherhood*
i *Comfort*
j *Power*
k *Contemplation*
l *Strength*
m *Death*
n *Remembrance*
14 b/w photographs
each 26.5 × 26.5 cm (10½ × 10½ in)
Artist's Collection, Munich
(*See Fig.79*)

53 Mick Rooney
Into the Hands of Strangers
1989
Acrylic/oil on paper
1.30 × 1.02 m (4 ft 3 in × 3 ft 4 in)
Gillian Raffles, London
(*Col.Fig.73*)

54 Mick Rooney
A Sound of Distant Thunder
1989
Oil on canvas
1.52 × 1.22 m (5 ft × 4 ft)
Artist's Collection, London

55 Mick Rooney
The Fugitives
1989
Acrylic/oil on paper
86.5 × 78.5 cm (34 × 31 in)
Private Collection, London

56 Ellen Rothenberg
The Combing Shawl
1993
Text of the *Diary of Anne Frank* printed on vellum, graphite, aluminium and steel brackets, 350 combs cast in various metals
1.83 × 1.07 × 2.44 m (6 ft × 3 ft 6 in × 8 ft)
Artist's Collection, Chicago
(*Col.Fig.66*)

57 Shirley Samberg
5 figures from *Wrappings* series
1985-93
a 1.83 m × 51 cm × 40.5 cm (6 ft × 1 ft 8 in × 1 ft 4 in)
b 1.80 m × 81 cm × 40.5 cm (5 ft 11 in × 2 ft 8 in × 1 ft 4 in)
c 1.63 m × 56 cm × 56 cm (5 ft 4 in × 1 ft 10 in × 1 ft 10 in)
d 1.83 m × 45.5 cm × 38 cm (6 ft × 1 ft 6 in × 1 ft 3 in)
e 2.13 m × 91.5 cm × 30.5 cm (7 ft × 3 ft × 1 ft)
Burlap
Artist's Collection, Long Island, USA
(*See Fig.74*)

58 Nancy Spero
The Jew's Whore
1990
Hand printing on wallpaper
c.3.66 m (12 ft) wide
Artist's Collection, New York
(*See Col.Fig.68 for related work*)

Select Bibliography

Books

Amishai-Maisels, Ziva, *Depiction and Interpretation: The Influence of the Holocaust on the Visual Arts*, Pergamon Press, Oxford, 1993.

Blatter, Janet and Milton, Sybil, *Art of the Holocaust*, Pan Books Ltd, London, 1982.

Costanza, Mary S. *The Living Witness: Art in the Concentration Camps and Ghettos*, The Free Press, New York and London, 1982.

Felstiner, Mary Lowenthal, *To Paint her Life: Charlotte Salomon in the Nazi Era*, Harper Collins, New York, 1994.

Friedlander, Saul (ed.), *Probing the Limits of Representation: Nazism and the Final Solution*, Harvard University Press, Cambridge, Mass. and London, 1992.

Friedlander, Saul, *Reflections of Nazism: An Essay on Kitsch and Death*, Indiana University Press, Bloomington and Indianapolis, 1993.

Green, Gerald, *The Artists of Terezin*, Hawthorn Books Inc, New York, 1978.

Hartman, Geoffrey (ed.), *Holocaust Remembrance: The Shapes of Memory*, Basil Blackwell Ltd, Cambridge, Mass. and Oxford, UK, 1994.

Kantor, Alfred, *The Book of Alfred Kantor: An Artist's Journal of the Holocaust*, Judy Piatkus (Publishers) Ltd, London, 1987.

Köppen, Manuel (ed.), *Kunst und Literatur nach Auschwitz*, Erich Schmidt Verlag, Berlin, 1993.

Milton, Sybil (ed.), *The Art of Jewish Children, Germany 1936-1941*, Allied Books Ltd, New York, 1989.

Milton, Sybil and Nowinsky, Ira, *In Fitting Memory: The Art and Politics of Holocaust Memorials*, Wayne University Press, 1992.

Spiegelman, Art, *Maus: A Survivor's Tale*, Penguin Books, London, 1987.

Spiegelman, Art, *Maus II: A Survivor's Tale*, Penguin Books, London, 1992.

Thompson, Vivian Alpert, *A Mission in Art: Recent Holocaust Works in America*, Mercer University Press, Macon, Georgia, 1988.

Toll, Nelly, *Without Surrender: Art of the Holocaust*, Philadelphia Running Press, 1978.

Volavkova, Hanna (ed.), *I never saw another butterfly. ..: Children's Drawings and Poems from Terezin Concentration Camp 1942-1944*, McGraw-Hill, New York, 1962.

Young, James E., *The Texture of Memory: Holocaust Memorials and Meaning*, Yale University Press, New Haven and London, 1993.

Exhibition Catalogues

Burnt Whole: Contemporay Artists Reflect Upon the Holocaust, Washington Project for the Arts, Washington DC, 1994.

Chagall to Kitaj: Jewish Experience in Twentieth Century Art, Barbican Art Gallery, London/Lund Humphries, London, 1990.

Gedenken und Denkmal: Entwürfe zur Erinnerung an die Deportation und Vernichtung der jüdischen Bevölkerung Berlins, Berlinische Galerie, Berlin, 1988/9.

Remembering for the Future: Original Drawings and Reproductions, by Victims of the Holocaust from Concentration Camps and Ghettos 1940-1945, RIBA, London, 1988.

Seeing through 'Paradise': Artists and the Terezin Concentration Camp, Massachusetts College of Art, Boston, 1991.

Spiritual Resistance: Art from Concentration Camps 1940-1945, A Selection of Drawings from the Collection of Kibbutz Lohamei Haghetaot, Israel, Union of American Hebrew Congregations, 1981 [US touring exhibition].

Steine des Anstosses: Nationalsozialismus und Zweiter Weltkrieg in Denkmalen 1945-1985, Museum für Hamburgerische Geschichte, Hamburg, 1985.

The Art of Memory: Holocaust Memorials in History, Jewish Museum, New York/Prestel Verlag, Munich/New York, 1994.

The Living Witness, Art in the Concentration Camps, Museum of American Jewish History, Philadelphia, 1978.

Where is Abel, Thy Brother?, National Gallery of Contemporary Art Zachęta, Warsaw, 1995.

Witness and Legacy: Contemporary Art about the Holocaust, Minnesota Museum of American Art, St Paul/Lerner Publications, Minneapolis, 1995.

Articles

Dabba Smith, Frank, 'Photography and the Holocaust', *Journal of Progressive Judaism*, No.1, November 1993.

Johnson, Ken, 'Art and Memory', *Art in America*, November 1993.

Milton, Sybil, 'Images of the Holocaust', *Holocaust & Genocide Studies*, Vol.I, Nos 1 and 2, 1986 [on photographs of the Holocaust].